Unbreakable

Becky —
Thank you for
reading my story!
Much gratitude —
Jasmine

Jasmine Rose Millwood

Wasteland Press

www.wastelandpress.net
Shelbyville, KY USA

Unbreakable
by Jasmine Rose Millwood

Copyright © 2012 Jasmine Rose Millwood
ALL RIGHTS RESERVED

First Printing – March 2012
ISBN: 978-1-60047-694-5

Printed in the U.S.A.

0   1   2   3   4   5   6   7   8   9   10   11

Dedicated to all the children still hiding in the shadows suffering from what I was so fortunate to escape. May an angel find you and carry you away soon.

To my beautiful and brave sisters—thank you for the strength not only to survive those two years, but also for the strength to share our story. Your love and support is the reason I have been able to accomplish this goal. I hope reading this helps you in a way that writing this helped me.

And most importantly, for my Uncle Richard, who rescued me, always guided me to make the right choices, and never gave up on me. I will never be able to fully show my gratitude for your unconditional love that helped make me the strong, independent woman that I am today.

Acknowledgements

I'd like to take a moment to give recognition to a few very special people who helped me lift this dream off the ground. I should tell you that two months before this book was published, I felt lost in this goal. I knew publishing this book was something I wanted to do, I just didn't know how to get there. The finish line was in sight but I needed a roadmap to make it to the end. Without these people and their support, encouragement, advice, and resources, I would have never been able to share my story with you.

To a very special man and his loving, compassionate wife who was not only my soccer coach when I was six, but he is the sole reason I was able to get this book on bookshelves. He extended many professional connections that each aided in reaching 'mini-goals' to get this big goal accomplished. He guided me to protect my work, and inspired me to create an enterprise based on my message. Rob Bilkie, you are an incredibly intelligent, inspiring and successful man that I will look up to from this day forward. You not only inspired me to take my memoir and transform it into a beautifully written book but also gave me the support I needed at an crucial time in my life. You and your wife, Shari, have become my good friends and I would still be lost behind that bar without your courage and faith in me.

To my publicist, Ashley Bilkie. Little did your dad know our relationship would transform into an incredibly strong and effective friendship. Not only have you been the most efficient publicist, but you also encouraged me to talk about something that I feel contains more shame than my childhood abuse—my eating disorder. I can only pray that someday I will be able to return the generosity and support you have given me while you strive to achieve your own endeavors.

To my editor, Alex Cruden. Thank you for doing the most difficult task of all—making this story into a book. What you did to my story while editing this book is much like what happened to my heart while writing it. You just put it back together. I knew it needed help, reconstruction, suggestions, deletions, and you did it all. Thank you for your utmost professionalism and commitment to help make my dream a reality.

My older sister Fawna…you may not think it at times, but you *did* protect us. You were—and still are—the best big sister a girl could ask for. You made sure we had food before you ate; you made sure you were getting the worst of it so that we didn't. You were brave enough to plan an escape, and that bravery has transpired to the stunning, compelling and fun-loving woman you are today. I am so glad you have found happiness; you earned it by protecting us when you were only a child yourself.

To my twin sister, Cam. We shared a womb, a bedroom, a life, and now only a birthday. Although we are sometimes referred to as night and day, we endured most of the things in our childhood as one. I'll never forget all the late night talks, how angry at you I was the day you moved out, and how happy I am that you finally understand that people love and accept you for who you are. You are a beautiful girl with so much potential. I'm proud to call such a creative and sweet girl my twin. No twins will ever share the special bond we have.

To a woman I not only look up to but am so lucky to call one of my best friends, Erika Smith. You have become such a close friend of mine, and the day I found out you read my book before anybody else had was the day I knew we'd be the best of friends forever. You gave me the provision and the confidence I so desperately needed. You are truly an amazing person and I thank God every day for putting you in my life. I am so thankful for your unconditional support and unreserved love—it was the missing piece I'd been searching for my whole life.

To my oldest and most endearing friend, Marianne Williamson. From the day you became my fellow 'Rustproofer' until you opened your heart to become an encouraging and supportive friend, I'll cherish your friendship forever. Thank you for reading my story, giving me feedback, sharing your thoughts, support and even your family.

To a more new friend but one I feel like I've known my whole life, Heather Chateauvert. Thank you for being instrumental in this exciting process by sharing your professional community and sharing your heart. Your support has been so generous, and your friendship means so much to me.

To my aunt, Debbie Collier who helped me accurately depict our life before my sisters and I were placed with my father. Thank you for helping me compose this section in the book and thank you for driving us far away from that prison that day. Thank you for being a mother-like figure and helping me prepare for the Miss Michigan pageant. You too, sacrificed much for my sisters and me and we are so grateful for all you have done.

To my cousins, Trisha and Belinda, who helped give me two weeks I'll never forget. You loved me when I needed nothing but love. You stroked my hair and kissed my head when I felt nothing but abandoned. Thank you for hugging me so tight, and thank you, Tee and Bea, for being two more big sisters that I needed to admire.

To my other aunt, Lynne Rohlfing, thank you for being the classy, stylish, and sophisticated woman you are. Even with your hands full you still gave us everything you could. Your hugs, kisses, your beautifully wrapped gifts, and most importantly, your perfume—helped instill a feminine potential that helped shape us into beautiful women. Thank you for hosting Christmas those first years we were out of my father's home, those were the holiday memories I'll remember forever.

To my cousins, aunts and uncles, little cousins, and grandparents. Thank you for believing in me and helping to guide me as I grew up to stay on track and make the right decisions. Timm Rohlfing, Jeff and Erin Rohlfing, Paul and Vicky Kolbe, Elizabeth and James Hensley, Jessica and Mike Legue, Melissa and Anthony Munaco, Aunt Elizabeth Treger.

To YMCA Storer Camps, the counselors who accepted a young girl they knew was struggling, to the friends I made there who taught me how to have healthy friendships, and to a special girl named Amelia Black. Attending Summer Camp those years showed me that it was possible to love and trust adults again. Amelia, I'll never forget the time we hid in the tent and cried so our parents wouldn't find us and take us home. You were one of the first friends to show me what a true friendship is. I'm proud to call such a beautiful and kindhearted woman one of my best friends.

To two special people that have bigger hearts than anyone I know, Stephanie and Mickey Hamilton. You were the foster parents we needed and just knowing you would have snatched us away from my father had you known the truth is comfort in itself. You were so kind and we would have been so lucky to spend our lives together.

To a few of my close friends who reminded me how strong and brave I was to do this, Elzabeth Elzey, Lindsay Burke, to the entire

Reaume Family, Christine Allen, Tony and Grace Gilmore, Pamela Ayres, Jenny Gilroy, Don Hawkins, Lynn & Jamesena Ingram and their three beautiful children, P.J., Joey and Penelope.

To Anita and John Farrar, for their support in editing the book and authoring the insightful and strong afterward. I am forever grateful for your friendship and kindness.

To my Uncle Richard, for rescuing me, loving me, and supporting me. I love you.

And lastly, to a man I love in a completely different way, Joshua Edgar. I promise this will be the only time I talk about you in this book. I would not have been able to do this without you standing by my side the whole time. Thank you for sitting next to me with your hand on my back as I wept while finishing this book. Thank you for driving me to that house in Brighton where I would have lost my composure without your holding my hand. Thank you for your advice, support, and motivation to accomplish a goal you knew all along was so important to me. And thank you for taking me to that pen shop, pulling out a piece of paper with a few pen names scribbled on it. As I looked at you in complete confusion (and annoyance) and you looked back at me with nothing but love and happiness in your eyes and said, "I want you to have a nice pen to sign your book with." The book hadn't even begun the editing stages but you insisted I have nothing but the best to leave my name in the flap. A gesture so genuine and thoughtful I'll think of every time I sign this book.

This book may be hard to follow or jumpy at times because emotions such as fear, anxiety, and confusion are evoked: the true emotions I felt not only while experiencing the situations described in this book, but also while writing about them later. Some of the events may be out of order because that is just how I remembered them. Please bear with me, as this story concludes with bright promise and unbridled potential.

Introduction

Growing up during such a tumultuous childhood helped mold me into a very strong person. One reason I was able to accept my past was because I was able to always lean on my sisters who lifted my chin up when I needed it most. The three of us are only as strong as those people who have webbed themselves around us to love, protect and respect us. In reflection of our past, I am grateful that many times in our lives we have been surrounded by that web. I am grateful for the people that have been my web to help me become someone special despite the extreme situations we were faced with and the simple fact that we were robbed of our childhoods.

But through it all Jasmine, Fawna and I, were able to bond together in times of abuse and and neglect that characterized the first twelve years of my life, as we clung together as a family because it was the only way to survive. My sisters have always been there for me and Jasmine specifically exemplifies a person I that I admire. She is a strong, honest, and kind woman and has only earned even more of my heart by putting this experience down on paper for the world to read. I can only hope that others read it and not only learn from society's mistakes but feel compelled to aid Jasmine in her mission of protect the children of the world from abuse and neglect.

Having my sister publish a book about the worst parts of our lives has changed my feelings on it for the better and helped me begin to heal and see that simply being alive is a feat, especially the three of us being alive together. For all of this and much more, I cannot thank her enough. I love you, Jasmine and Fawna.

Camai Millwood

As a child I always had a great imagination and creative personality. Most people thought that I dreamt of things like graduating high school, attending college, finding my career, wedding day, future husband, and children that I wanted of my own. However, in the middle of my childhood years I never envisioned my life beyond what my sisters and I called "hell." These two years that we spent fighting for each other, our lives and our childhood, I could only see the three of us growing up and hating the world or even worse, one day *her* going too far and killing us.

This horrible thought process all changed the day I realized I was going to graduate high school, attend college, and find my career. I realized that my life was not over—but rather just beginning. The lives we now have are lives that I had never envisioned. Every milestone that I have been able to accomplish in my life has been one of those distant dreams come true. Our bond as sisters was compromised at times but throughout the years we continue to share something very special in common: our survival and empowerment.

Every day I am thankful for our family that helped support us in our recovery phase, whether they knew how much we needed them or not. I am thankful for my Uncle Richard, for stepping up and caring for us when we felt that we had no one on our side. I deeply admire him for taking in three girls, to raise as his own, each with severe emotional baggage. Not only did he raise us but from day one he would never let us feel sorry for ourselves—something I attribute to our self-drive and determination. He would encourage us to be involved with our community, be active members of society, and stay friends only with people who treat us with respect. I know deep down

I will forever be grateful to him for being stepping up and being the parent we needed when we had none.

This book tells our story about our true and honest struggles that the three of us faced on a daily basis. Being the oldest, my memories of these situations are more vivid than my sisters, which is why the three of us sharing what we remember collectively has made such a real depiction of the most terrible time in our lives. What happened to us behind those closed doors is our true story that our family, friends, coaches and mentors need to know. It is our hope that those social workers, principals and teachers who failed to act on our behalf will learn from our story and realize the effects their shortcomings had. Knowledge is power and knowing the signs, severity, and repercussions of child abuse based on our own sobering story may one day help save an innocent child's life or empower an abused child to stand up and speak out against attackers. I support my little sister, Rosie (my nickname for Jasmine), for her strength to not only write our story but to finally share it with the world. Thank you, Jasmine, for finally doing something we have talked about for years. Your courage and bravery will take you as far as you can dream. You are the perfect example of not allowing a past to define you or your future. I love you both.

Fawna Millwood

A Pageant Girl

As I stand here waiting behind the heavy black curtain, I regret my decision to ever do this. "I am so stupid," I mumble to myself. The thick, dark fabric of the curtain shields me from the world, yet on the other side shines the opportunity to unveil myself as a newly accomplished and beautiful young woman. My heart is thumping almost out of my chest, and my breaths are quick and shallow. I want to just turn around, find my way down to the dressing room, and pretend as if I never even decided to do this in the first place. The announcer roars the name of the contestant in front of me and I begin to feel as if I'm going to pass out. I know all of my closest friends and family are sitting in the audience, along with hundreds of other strangers. I know they are all anxiously waiting for me to walk out from behind the curtain and show my face to the world.

"I can't do this; there is no way. How did I think I have enough courage to walk out in front of hundreds of people in my bikini and heels?" This is a nightmare come true. "But I've lived real nightmares," I think to myself. Even so, I begin to break out into a cold sweat and feel flutters in my heart worse than before.

"Jasmine Millwood, Miss Plymouth USA!" the announcer roars. The audience goes wild, and based on the amplitude of the applause I feel as if every person there is cheering for me. I take a step out into the hot spotlight and feel dizzy. The air feels stuffy and I'm smiling into pure blackness. Every emotion possible is racking my brain. I don't know whether to cry or laugh or fall to the floor and pretend I'm dead. This could quite possibly be every woman's worst nightmare with the addition of a few inches of material and a pair of sparkling silver five-inch heels.

I somehow have enough strength to trudge to front stage with a gleaming smile. My knees feel weak yet I start to feel a power in my soul I never felt before. I glide over to left stage with a stylish French turn and flash my big smile and sparkling white teeth to the crowd. I hear whistles and clapping and feel a rush of relief. "You're halfway there, Jasmine, come on, stand up straight, keep smiling, you can do this." I remember the countless hours of pageant training, and my pageant trainer hounding me about keeping my legs together and pinching a quarter with my shoulder blades. I knew she was sitting in one of the front rows but I couldn't feel the courage yet to look for her. Big hair, bold eyes, firm butt. I really didn't want to let her down. I didn't want to let anyone down. I especially didn't want to let myself down.

I walk to right stage and do an elegant pivot on the disc. I can feel everyone watching me and evaluating every curve on my body and every move on the stage. My legs are so tense I can feel a bad cramp lingering. My eyes dart an assurance of confidence but also a sense of fear to the judges in the front row. I want them to feel inferior and astonished by a charisma I am so badly trying to convey. I begin to emulate a sense of confidence and charm, losing all fear and anxiety. I hold my head up and smile big. Although my feet are screaming for relief from the previous 48 hours of rehearsal, my legs still glide across the stage with a now-present alluring sway in my hourglass-shaped hips.

I am at the 2008 Miss Michigan USA Pageant. I take my first breath since I first walked out on stage and start to melt. My body finally feels a sense of limberness and my eyes transform into convincing darts of passion and confidence. Each step I take, from that moment on, is a stomp on every person who told me I would never become anyone. Every smile I flash is a burst closer to the dreams I am about to envision. Each sparkle in my eyes is an explosion to the woman who called me ugly every day for two years.

I glide to left stage, make my last mark and flash the biggest smile I have ever flashed. I feel like I am dripping sweat but still ice cold to the touch. I also feel like a queen, in charge of the world and everyone in it. I feel worthy.

I gracefully make my way off the stage and my knees immediately go weak. I feel a rush of success and triumph. The other contestants gather all around and begin chattering about their highs of adrenaline. I stand by myself for a few moments to take in what I had just done. But taking in my performance on stage only serves to reveal a very long and turbulent journey as to how I got here.

I picture the day, when I was six years old, that the social workers ripped my sisters and me away from my Uncle Richard, who loved us more than anyone did. I picture us crying and clinging to him in confusion and anger. I see flashbacks of moments scattered throughout the two horrid years with my stepmother and father, where we came so close to death many times from starvation and never-ending violent abuse. I see her standing in my face as I beg for mercy, and she tells me I am so ugly she can't even look at me.

I see the afternoon that I learn of my adoption, and how mad I was at my uncle for surrendering any opportunity I might have for a normal mom-and-dad life. I hated that day, where I had no self-esteem, no understanding, and no voice. Then I see myself in middle school, with my relentless pre-teen female classmates gossiping about my Salvation Army wardrobe and ridiculous attempt to wear blue eyeliner. I think about the years I spent just wondering how much different a woman I would have become with a mother to guide me. I remember my first kiss and my first break-up, and how my uncle didn't know how to console me so he brought me a red balloon.

I think about the dozens of different homes I was put in, just like a doll in a dollhouse. I see my little four-year old self with blonde hair and green eyes and how I felt for most of my life that nobody loved me.

As my recollections flash back and forth across the years, I also see my relatives that continued to fight for me, and the face of the man who took advantage of me when I was five years old. I see the teachers who did and did not believe in me, and all the therapists and their sad sympathetic eyes. I see my amazing sisters and how we got through it all together. I see the day we were taken away from our biological father and that criminal of a stepmother, and my last memory of him is the fake tears in his big green eyes.

I see the days at the Orchards Foster Care Agency and all the supervised visits, my own mother crying as we sat around a child-size plastic table and her begging me to tell the judge that we want to live with her despite her obvious inability to care for us in the slightest way. I remember all the nights I slept on her kitchen floor in Romulus with a newspaper as my sheets next to a pile of ants and stale cereal. I quickly realize I went from a low of huddling on a cold, dark tile floor to standing tall on the brightly lit stage of the Miss Michigan pageant.

This last thought snaps me back to reality, where I see the other girls now calmly collected and feeling accomplished. I think to myself, "I can't believe I just did that." I can see the audience through gaps in the curtain and I have never felt more worthy. My courage and determination brought me here, and nothing—not anything—will bring me back.

I follow the rest of the contestants backstage and try hard to contain the mix of emotions. Tears flush down my face and my stage makeup begins to droop. I had been such a tough girl up until now. I had always been blatantly open about my past and the things that happened to me, but at this moment a rush of emotions runs through me that no wall could withstand. The other girls look confused and helpless as I stand there and cry about what I had just done. No, I didn't win that contest. But I became stronger by trying.

When people find out I competed in beauty pageants, the general reaction is usually: "Oh, so you're a pageant girl, then?" And to those people my reply is: If by a pageant girl you mean I had enough courage to put on a tiny bikini and five-inch heels and walk on a stage in front of all my closest friends and family, and the whole world for that matter, then yes. I had enough determination to go through months of pageant training where I learned how to walk with feminine grace and carry myself with confidence. I had enough determination to throw an eating disorder out the window and work out at the gym for two hours, every day, for five months. I watched my diet, learned about current events, became a charming and intelligent woman with goals. I learned that not all relationships are healthy, even if it hurts to cut the rope. I became immersed in a platform that spoke to me: abused and neglected children and foster care. I was able to continue writing a book that I had begun nine years prior, and with the courage the pageant provided me I have been able to finish that story and make it be available for the world to read.

So my response to those people is: Yes, I am a pageant girl. I did all of that. I became someone. And that someone helped get me to where I am today, with the strength and courage to share something with you so close to my heart.

The following email was the last contact I had with my biological father. He had his own parental rights terminated not even a year after being removed from his custody and I had no contact with him until I turned 18.

After receiving his email, I first thought some pretty angry thoughts, calmed down and felt a slight sadness, and then permanently erased him from my memories, my life, and my heart. I'm sharing it with you so you understand why I have been able to forgive. And why I will never be able to forget. Goodbye Benjamin.

January 7, 2007

Hey Girls- I just want you to know I'm thinking about you all, I can't even tell you how proud I am of you, and that I love you all VERY much. I was just with a friend, talking, and it re-hashed a lot of feelings and crap that happened. He told me that everything happens for a reason. I've been trying to tell myself that since my decision was made, but it never made up for what was lost. I have so much I want to tell you girls, I just want to know you'll listen, and THEN judge. There's always two sides to every story, and Jasmine, you really should've interviewed me before you sent your book to the publishers. I know what I did, and it was wrong. So now I will continue my life knowing I screwed up big time, but you should know that none of you would be where you are right now if I didn't make that decision. I'm not looking for any kudos, Lord know, I don't deserve them, but I just want you to know I love you all. Love Dad

At the time that my father sent this email, he knew I was writing a book but didn't realize I hadn't published it yet. In retrospect, I see this email as a blessing in disguise. Although it was painful to finally realize I'll never have my real dad in my life, at last I knew the answer to a question I had been asking myself for years. Did he know what happened when he wasn't home? Did he know how scared, hungry, and desolate we were? Did he know what she did to us?

The answer? He knew. He knew every detail described in this book. He knew that we cried, and begged, and prayed for a better life, every day for two years. The problem was, he had this woman in his life that he loved more than us. He wanted to make her happy. He chose her. You know what, Benjamin, you're right. There are two sides in every story. And in this story, there is right and there is wrong. And what happened in this story is wrong.

It is as simple as that. My father is a coward. And because of his actions he made and for even remotely thinking he deserves credit for any of them, he will never know the incredible daughters he so easily gave away that cloudy and colder-than-normal June morning.

Why This Book Exists

2

You should know I have three reasons behind publishing this book. First and most importantly, I want this to be a book that provides support and hope for other victims. Either current or past, victims need to know they are not alone in their suffering. It is my hope that anyone in similar pain should use this book as proof that life can get better. Whether it is a new parent learning different ways to discipline a child, or a child crying out for help, or just a regular person trying to find comfort, I hope this book serves as a common ground for us to all find a fellow survivor and survive.

Secondly, this book marks an accomplishment that I have been dreaming of for fourteen years. Writing this book empowered me to heal on my own. I had to see it through from my bedside to the bookshelf because I started from nothing and became something, and I hope my book does the same.

Lastly, I'm publishing this book for my sisters. Our voice is so much louder when we speak in sync and, on behalf of them, I say that although we are vulnerable and still may feel shame from time to time, we feel honored to share our story with you.

When I started to piece this book together, I had trouble making it into a readable story. The manuscript had no flow; it was broken and hard to follow. You see, this book began as a collection of nightmares I'd been having in the first few years out of my father's custody. I'd wake up in the middle of the night shaking, barely able to catch my breath, thinking I was back *there*. As soon as I regained consciousness and realized it was all just a horrible dream, I would write down my recollections into what soon became a journal. This journal developed into my own self-therapy and I began to realize that this therapy per se was helping me put my past to rest and start living a happier life.

That ten-year-old girl who had the life beaten and starved out of her died in that house. And by putting my pen to paper in the wee hours of the night, that ten-year-old girl came alive.

To finish the book—to find the strength to relive and share my story—I decided I needed one last trip back to the house where my sisters and I were nearly killed. So on a cold and cloudy October day I drove to Brighton to find this strength I so badly needed to make my dream a reality. The whole way there I contemplated turning around, thinking the house might not still be there, there might be a new happy family now living there, or that the trip was all just a waste of gas. But I continued to drive along, passing the beautiful fall trees and countless pumpkins on porches, in a quest to catch a glimpse of the house where it all happened. I pulled into downtown Brighton and drove past all the small shops and little cafes. My heart began to thump loud. I turned the radio off and took a deep breath. I wondered if the school was still there—the school that knew so much and did so little.

Ahead of me are the railroad tracks that brought a rattling to our home every night with a roaring train that I always wished so badly I could jump on to get far, far away from this place. I drive on and see the drooping mulberry tree that hung its branches in the same way I hung my head for two years. And then, before I know it, there it is. The big, white, rickety old house with ghastly memories only five people ever knew—until now. It stands powerful and strong but looks older than I remember. I begin to shake and can't seem to breathe. There it stands, staring at me, whispering loudly, "How dare you come back here."

Tears fall from my eyes as I stare back at this monstrosity, thanking God for letting me live and also hating him at the same time for putting me through all that. I envision the inside, with fake wood panels lining the interior, the old furniture, the prickly carpet I was pushed down to, the sink where my little hands were scalded, the bedroom where I prayed for my sisters to still be alive when I was allowed to come out, the bathroom where I lay in my own blood for hours. Just looking at the house brings on physical pain; yet, at the same time, I also begin to feel a sense of liberation that I was able to come here and face the house that almost killed me.

I continue to stand on the sidewalk in front of the house. It looms over me, but now I have more dignity. I shift my weight to a more powerful stance and say out loud, "I know you wanted me dead, but I am still here, alive, strong, beautiful."

I wonder if the people who live there now know that innocent children screamed and cried in their house every day for two long years. I wonder how anyone could feel happy living there. I think about going inside but decide that just coming here is the closure I need to continue on my writing journey. I sob, haunted by the memories that I knew would have to be part of this book.

The only thing that gives me enough strength to turn away is the realization that soon the whole world would know the very things this house knows. I realize that I have to publish this book so everyone would finally know the truth. Yes, when my sisters and I were younger we thought we had to lie. Yes, we told the social workers what happened, and they did nothing. So, we started telling the social workers nothing wrong was happening. Yes, even after we left this house we didn't want to believe the horrors we endured were real. But now, as I walk away from the house and realize the whole world will know the truth, I feel it crumble behind me.

Understanding How
We Got There

3

On March 28, 1988, in a small hospital in
Anchorage, Alaska, my biological mother gave birth to two jaundice-
stricken and premature but otherwise healthy twin girls. Preceded by
a happy and healthy two-years-older sister named Fawna, the twins
remained in the neo-natal ICU for five weeks as they grew to normal
birth weight and developed into healthy infants. We were named
Jasmine, after the flower, and Camai, (pronounced Sha-my), which
means a "warm and genuine hello" in the Yup'ik language, which
stems from the Eskimo-Aleut language commonly spoken in south-
central Alaska.

My biological mother had already begun a life dabbling in
common drugs (including prescription drugs) and sometimes alcohol,
and even after the birth of the twins this was a life she continued to
choose. My father was also now accompanying her with drug usage
and binge drinking. Sometimes my grandmother cared for us while
my mother and father went out on these late-night extravaganzas, but
caring for three little girls with health problems and bad colic was
soon becoming too much for her to handle.

My mother's drug problem, combined with an undiagnosed
bipolar disorder called manic depression, forced my father to rethink
his marriage. He was slowly distancing himself from her as he decided
to move back to Michigan to live with my aunt, who was helping to

support him in hopes he would get on his feet and step up take care of his children. Little did she know that was never part of his plan.

Soon the relationship between my mother and father became filled with tension, and in the end, the three of us were the ones who suffered. After my father left, my mother's problems multiplied: a failed marriage, three children she didn't want, and nobody to help her take care of them. Her role as our mother and sole caretaker was dwindling as we were growing older and needed more care. Her drug use increased as she refused to take any responsibility for her children. My grandmother soon phoned my aunt in Michigan, who immediately flew to Anchorage to take us home. When my aunt arrived, she saw three girls who desperately needed medical attention, food, and, most importantly, love.

My aunt then flew us back to Michigan where she began to care for us. At this time my father was nowhere to be found. We were on a path to a happy childhood and a stable home. But a few months later, my unstable mother notified local authorities to report her children had been kidnapped in an attempt to make her look like the victim. On December 21, 1988, my aunt pulled in her driveway after work and was surrounded by the local police, the FBI, and a child abduction agency. They demanded my aunt surrender the twins (Fawna was not requested, as my mother had previously signed her guardianship over to my aunt). We were flown back up to Alaska, where news reports showed my mother happily being reunited with her girls.

In February of 1989 my grandmother called my aunt, yet another time, to ask that my aunt take us back to Michigan (again), but this time per my own mother's request. Court documents show my mother going as far as to state, "You need to come get Jasmine. Her colic is so bad I'm going to put her up for adoption."

My aunt bought plane tickets for everyone, including my mother, to bring us all home to Michigan. But when she arrived in Alaska, we were nowhere to be found. After she drove around for hours looking for us, we were finally located in a rundown trailer that my aunt later described as a nightmare. Reports show that Cam and I were found lying on a dirty, bare mattress, in our own feces and urine, and pus oozed out of my left ear from a punctured eardrum. My mother had completely lost any desire to care for her children and had chosen a life filled with drugs and alcohol over three girls that desperately needed her.

At the airport, while Camai and I waited with my aunt to board the plane, my aunt was paged. It was my mother. She told my aunt that she just couldn't go to Michigan and that she was required to go to court in Alaska on a shoplifting charge. She requested that my aunt please take us to Michigan. So, my aunt boarded the plane with Cam and I in hopes of continuing the life she had started for us since she found out the situation in the beginning. Upon returning home, my aunt was given financial support from my Uncle Richard and grandfather for cribs and my Aunt Lynne pitched in for money for clothes. It was finally a happy reunion and we were almost ready to start that new happy life, just a little later.

It wasn't long before the Orchards Children's Services in Southfield, Michigan, got involved and began to facilitate the custody arrangements for us girls after my mother decided she wanted to be a mom again. We were placed with her for a short while and then moved into a foster home when she was deemed unfit to care for us. She was instructed to prove that she could provide a stable environment for us to live in. After we bounced around between foster homes, my Uncle Richards, and my mother's for a few years, the State of Michigan awarded my mother custody of us again. She was clean at the time we moved in, only to revert back to her irresponsible parenting and drug-using soon after. Drug dealers and boyfriends came to and left the apartment in Romulus as we were desperate for food and care.

We were placed back into foster care, where we bounced around to a few more families who never wanted all three of us at the same time. We were forced to separate. Some of the foster families were nice, others not so much. I remember one home where the foster parents were so old they could hardly even walk up stairs. One family I was with for a short period was rigidly strict and my foster mother was violent at times. She dragged me around by my ear and screamed at me to do chores with the rest of the children.

One foster family we lived with for an unusually extended period was a couple my sisters and I refer to as "Stephanie and Mick." They were so generous and compassionate, as they agreed to take all of us at once. Although I was young while in their care I remember they were more loving than anyone else. They provided us with food, shelter, and, most importantly, affection. I will never forget their compassion and the sacrifices they made for my sisters and me. Court documents reveal a fierce battle occurring between my mother and my fostermom, Stephanie. Stephanie filed a petition to keep us but my mother wouldn't allow it. She accused my fostermom of "planning to kidnap the children" and "being overbearing and offensive." We were soon taken away from Stephanie and Mick, one of the saddest days in our lives until that point.

At the time a social worker informed me that we were, yet again, going to be put back with my mother, I was a little excited to think of us as a "family" again. The fact that my mother was actually fighting for me made me feel happy and loved. I didn't care that she was a bad parent because I knew I would have Fawna to take care of me. I was getting older and realizing how much I needed my mom.

We were placed back with my mother for the final time when I was five years old. I was in kindergarten and had begun to form some of my earliest complete memories. My mother had now—by actions only of her own—completely lost control of us and we fended for ourselves every day. Sometimes, in severe depression, she would stay in bed for weeks a time. At other times, in severe mood swings, she would scream and cry while my sisters and I wept in confusion and distress.

My father would sometimes visit, and I loved it when he did. He always cooked us food and played games with us. I hoped he and my mother would work things out but they never did. The screaming and fighting between them during his visits was almost unbearable. She was now doing more drugs than ever, and her broken promises had become broken records.

Fawna assumed the mother role in a way nobody else would ever seem to be able to do. She took care of us first, then herself. She helped get us ready for school (I hated when she brushed my hair), packed our lunches, zipped up our jackets, and walked us to school. She waited for us at the end of the school day to walk us home. I was jealous of her because my father took her to a daddy-daughter dance and I wanted it to be me. But I still loved her and was grateful she took care of Cam and me.

My aunt remembers coming to visit us about three months after we had been living with my mother this time and depicts almost unimaginable conditions. Social workers came on their next visit and noted Fawna (age seven) frying bacon on the stove and me (age five) making coffee to serve to my mother, who was passed out in bed after another drug binge. I remember this time vividly because it was the beginning of a life where I would be forced to be older than the age I really was. Soon my life demanded I mature and be an adult, starting at the early and innocent age of five.

One of the most devastating and frightening things that happened during this period is hard for me to talk about. I tried to block it from my memory, but I could not help but realize how it was yet another time that social workers and adults failed us yet again. One of my mother's so-called friends began inappropriately touching me while my mother was gone or passed out in her bed. I felt violated and had nobody to turn to. The sexual abuse never went beyond this inappropriate touching, but when I tried to tell a therapist that it was happening she didn't listen. She told me I that did not understand what was happening, and to accuse someone of doing this was a very serious allegation. I understood that what that man was doing was wrong. I cried myself to sleep many nights praying someone would help me stop him from doing it again. It was a dark time in my life, but just the beginning of a long road of adversity to face in the short childhood I had left.

Social workers were coming to check on us a lot now and I could tell they were never really satisfied. Once a social worker pointed under the kitchen table and asked if that was where I slept, and I didn't know what to answer because I didn't want to get my mom in trouble. They spoke with my mother every time and she cried and begged for them not to take us away. They demanded that she get clean of drugs in order to keep us, but it finally became clear that her drug life was more important to her than her own three daughters. We were taken away from her for the last time in the summer of 1994.

We were placed back into foster homes and began acting out. Our caseworker at the time noted we had begun lying, throwing temper tantrums and causing trouble. Documents also indicate I had begun displaying textbook signs of sexual abuse and become overly friendly towards adult males. I was, however, very sensitive to being left alone with them. After a foster parent I was living with at the time requested an investigation be opened, social workers began slowly trying to pinpoint the perpetrator and the crime. After three months of therapy I had finally identified my offender and the police soon got involved. A few months later, the investigation was closed as prosecutors determined I was "too young and would not testify." I don't remember ever telling anyone I would not testify.

During all of this time that we bounced around to dozens of different homes, my father was still drinking and reportedly telling social workers he was "unable to plan for his children at this time." He also spent three months incarcerated in the Oakland County Jail for a DUI. His lack of responsibility or any financial contribution continued on for six years.

My Uncle Richard offered to let us live with him again until we found a more stable home or until my mother became sober. His job required him to work a lot and he didn't have much help, but he made sure our life was good. We were fed healthy meals; they didn't always taste good but at least were nutritious. He got us involved with soccer, and he let us watch cartoons. He had a lot of rules that, naturally, as kids, we didn't want to obey, but it certainly wasn't terrible living there. It was a pretty good life.

I was making some friends (when I wasn't being asked, "Where's Aladdin?" or "How come you live with your uncle?") and getting used to a stable environment. We were beginning to like school, and we loved that by living with him we were also in contact with our extended family. We grew close with our cousins, aunts, and uncles. That year that we lived with Uncle Richard was one of the best years of my childhood. On Christmas Eve of 1995 my Aunt Lynne and Uncle Bill had the family over for the holiday, and my sisters and I spent hours sledding down a huge hill in their backyard, "snowjumping" as we called it. It was one of the happiest days of my young life.

During the spring of 1995 my father began visiting us more often. He and my Uncle Richard typically got along. Court documents show that my father was nowhere to be found for the first six years of my life until one day he had decided out of the blue that he wanted us girls. Caseworkers were relieved that he finally decided to step up, as my mother was nowhere near suitable as a parent. My father soon explained to us that he had met this woman who we were really going to love. That previous Christmas she even gave the three of us gifts. Mine was a big pillow with Minnie Mouse on it. I liked her already and I didn't even know her.

The idea of leaving our "strict Uncle Richard" to live with our real dad and what could be a stable and nurturing mother was appealing. We quickly agreed to this alluring idea when the social workers asked us how we felt about moving in with them. Since the social service system always attempts reunification with the biological parents before resorting to alternatives, moving in with our father and his deceivingly beautiful, sweet, and loving girlfriend was only a few short weeks away.

While filling in the blanks of my life story I should explain what has become of the relationship between my mother and me. I know in my heart she loves my sisters and me. I know she tried sometimes (maybe not hard enough) to care for us as best she could. It took me a long time to accept it, but she really is sick. Manic depression is a serious bi-polar disorder that requires several medications and ongoing, intense therapy. And despite her illness, however, she never, not ever, laid a hand on us. If there was anything we needed and she was sober enough to provide it, she would. But here is the bottom line. She let us down too many times. She broke promise after promise, and her failures are part of the reason our childhoods were so arduous. She broke my heart and the hearts of my sisters. She chose a life where drugs and an addiction were more important than the daughters who desperately needed her at a trying time in their lives, especially as they were becoming women.

Therefore, I have chosen, just like the decision regarding my father, that although I long for a loving, understanding relationship with her, it is just not a possibility. Trust me, I would love to have a mother in my life. I want a mom to watch me try on my wedding dress and a mom to be the spoiling grandmother of my children. But being a parent does not guarantee you will be a good mother or father or deserving of raising children. I feel that there is a reason her rights were terminated by the state and why on my birth certificate, at the space for "mother," it is blank.

Because my life is now about protecting myself and my sisters, I must take her out of my life and keep her there. Children of parents who choose drugs over them would probably agree that their parents may have been sober in the past, or they may be sober now, but there might not be a time in the future when they are still sober. I refuse to set myself up for failure and heartbreak again.

A good quote I think helps explain this is, "It is much easier to ask another adult for help than a child for forgiveness." As my mother relentlessly continues to reach out to me and ask me to let her be a part of my life, I hear only one recurring theme: *I* want to be part of your life, *I* want to be your mom, *I* am really sober this time. I don't care if you are sober this time. If you haven't been able to understand by now, a mother-daughter relationship doesn't revolve around one person. You chose *you* too many times and now it is time for me to choose a healthy me.

Falling into a Hellhole 4

When we were first getting to know Diane, things were actually really great. I was such a happy kid. I finally felt normal, getting ready to live with two parents—a mom and a dad—in a nice house while going to a nice school. Diane seemed beautiful to me. I could tell my father really cared about her. He picked her up a lot and she would wrap her legs around him while they started to passionately kiss. This never bothered me because I liked seeing my dad so happy. I liked seeing this kind of love. He smiled so much around her, and it made me smile to see that happiness in him. She had big teeth that sparkled and a big smile most of the time.

Although this was going to be her first experience raising children, I truly felt that she was trying her best to be a mom. My sisters and I were so relieved we didn't have to deal with our real mom and the never-ending false guarantees or have to bounce around to and from foster families anymore. We finally had a sense of belonging.

We met Diane during the winter of 1994, about six months before we all began living together. We were living with our uncle during this time. Uncle Richard was pretty strict but fed us ice cream with cereal on top (that was his favorite treat to give us) and let us watch television. We played outside, rode bikes, and loved school. I loved my first-grade teacher, who showed me more affection and consistency than any adult ever had until that point. My favorite book was "The Berenstain Bears' New Baby," my favorite color was cerulean (that was so like me to pick favorite things that were unique), and I desperately—like any other girl my age—wanted a baby kitten more than anything.

It was the very instant we moved into the house that Diane's attitude toward us changed. It was as if she had been putting on an act just to get us to move in with my dad and her. So we did our own thing every day by playing outside and laughing and giggling. But she didn't like it when we had fun. She would yell at us and tell us that since we were bad that day we weren't allowed to have fun. This became an every-day routine. She started taking away our toys one by one and hiding them. The problem was we were never really doing anything bad.

I soon realized that she never liked us from the beginning. When our dad would come home from work late in the evening, she would tell him we were bad or disrespectful. Diane was now telling us every day that we were rotten kids, and we were very slowly beginning to believe her.

Because Diane insisted on reporting back to my father every day that we were bad kids or were troublemakers since he had left, we were ordered to start sitting in our rooms. No television, no music, no toys. Just sitting. We stared at the walls and the windows, and if we were lucky enough very quietly whispered to each other and sometimes got teared-up wondering what we had done to not be allowed to play. This soon became the default to occupy our time. Just sitting.

Soon a common punishment became having to write the same sentence over and over until it filled up 20 pages. Whatever I was charged with doing, they would make a sentence out of it, and I would go in my room and write for hours. Soon I began spending the entire time I came home from school all the way until my father got home from work serving my punishment by writing out lines like, "I will not give Diane bad looks," or "I will not ruin other people's lives." My hand cramped up after the first few lines but I never stopped writing. I was scared to stop.

Diane sometimes told me to write until it was time for bed, often missing dinner. She would walk into my room and pages of paper would be sprawled across the floor. Soon my hand cramps started to go away and I could write for hours without it hurting. When she walked into my room I would immediately seek her approval by showing her the 20 pages of the same sentence written over a thousand times. She would just shake her head and walk out.

My sisters and I began to feel a slight fear of Diane. We were scared to say anything or even ask for food or water. We were afraid that she might start yelling at us and have our dad spank us when he got home. It went from bad to worse—and before we knew it, our lives were about to completely change.

It was a cool September afternoon. My sisters and I had gotten home from school a few hours earlier. We ate half of a peanut butter and jelly sandwich each and were told to sit in our rooms until our dad got home. I had a field trip permission slip from school that I needed to have an adult sign. Dad wasn't home from work yet so I asked Diane if she could do it for me. Diane was sitting in front of the television when I asked her. She quickly snatched the paper out of my hand, startling me. I jumped back a few inches and she snapped her head up and said, "What, are you scared of me or something?"

I quickly buckled my head down toward the floor and replied, "No Diane, I'm not scared of you…" in a little innocent voice, trying to figure out if I "gave her a bad look."

Diane stood up and set the piece of paper down on the chair. She snarled, "Look at me when I'm talking to you!" The moment I lifted my chin to her waist-level I felt her fist slam into the side of my head. It felt like someone had taken a rock and sling-shot it into my brain. Instantly I fell to the floor. Tears filled my eyes. I looked up at her as she barked without any emotion, "Your dad will do this when he gets home. Now go to your room!"

Quickly I stood up but almost fell from the throbbing pain next to my ear. It burned and pounded with every throb. I was a little dizzy but tried to remain focused on returning to my room as quickly as possible in case she felt the need to do something like that again.

I stumbled into my room and grabbed the wooden frame of my bunk bed to keep myself from falling over. I couldn't see because my eyes were welled up with tears and my vision became more blurry as the dizziness became more intense. I sat down on the bed and held the side of my head. I just felt shocked. I was so confused by what had just happened. I had done exactly what my teacher told me to do. I didn't understand why I was punished.

I sat in my room for a couple of hours. After the time passed and my headache began to dissipate my ears perked up when I heard a familiar sound. I could hear dishes clanging in the kitchen. I was beginning to think that maybe my punishment was over. I heard some glasses and dishware being set on the table, and I smiled. It was dinnertime; it was definitely time for me to come out of my room. Everyone will forgive each other. I also realized I was starving. I heard one of my sisters laughing but I didn't know what about. "They must be laughing about me," I thought.

I stood up and walked over to my door. I put my ear up, thinking Diane was going to send one of my sisters to come get me. But she never did. I almost gained enough courage to yell Diane's name in case she had just forgotten about me. But I sat alone, in the dark, with a faint headache and big heartache the rest of the night.

My dad came home from work late that night. I'm not sure what exactly Diane told him about what happened. Whatever it was, it wasn't in my favor. My dad came into my room. My heart jumped because I thought he was going to save me. But his eyes shot at me like missiles. I knew at that moment Diane had turned on me.

He stared me down as he walked closer and said, "Jasmine, were you a bad girl today?" I lifted my heavy head up as more tears filled my eyes and said, "No, Dad, I wasn't bad. I promise!" I pleaded. I thought he would be on my side. I was wrong. He then said, "You know what happens to kids when they are bad." I started to tremble when I looked up at him. He glared at me and signaled for me to bend over on his lap. He spanked me harder than I had ever been spanked before. I yelped and squirmed. I cried, from both the pain and the frustration.

I just didn't understand what I had done to deserve this. It just wasn't fair. I cried myself to sleep after my spanking. And that was it—the beginning of the disappearance of our chance for happy childhoods.

Instances such as those became a regular occurrence. Not just with me but also with my sisters. Diane began hitting us more frequently, grabbing our chins tightly and throwing us to the ground. We never did anything wrong like draw on the walls with crayon or refuse to clean up our toys. It was because we gave her a "bad look" or asked her for something to eat because we had gone hours without food. She hit us harder each time. She'd send us to our rooms with no dinner and send us to school with no breakfast or even a lunch.

When our dad would come home from work, she would tell him we were disrespectful and had disobeyed her polite requests. He would then spank us until we couldn't even sit down. He really loved her. He would believe anything she said about us. She got a sense of pleasure out of tormenting us in this way and seemed to thrive on watching us cry and whimper. Any sort of close relationship or bond we once shared with her was now gone. She was the woman who hit my sisters and me, went hours or days without feeding us, and had now turned our dad against us. That was all she was to us.

It wasn't long before she began to devise more ways to torment us. She found joy in sending us to school in the most outrageous outfits. She loved that the most: dressing us up in the most ridiculous, humiliating ensembles. One of only three pictures I have of myself during those two years is a photo taken on February 26, 1996. I was in second grade and standing up against a cold brick wall as my teacher snapped a Polaroid for a class project. I wore a dress that had my humiliation all over it. It was navy blue with giant pink and white flowers proudly parading throughout the fabric, accentuated with sleeves that puffed up like clouds. Kids laughed and poked fun at me all day long—and she knew it. I remember walking into school one day, and my teacher just burst out laughing. I tried so hard to hold my tears back. This life, why? What did we do to deserve this?

Diane loved to dress us the opposite of the weather. She'd send us to school in the hot months in layers of sweaters and heavy jeans. In the winter it was rarely a coat.

One day, she bashed me around the house until I couldn't breathe or feel my body. Then she rammed me into the bathroom and threw me onto the sink. With scissors, she quickly snipped my bangs in one motion to reveal sad, hopeless eyes and a bruised and puffy red face. I remember looking into the mirror, seeing blood, sweat, and her. Tears welled up in my eyes as I glanced down at my shiny blonde locks covering the sink, and I thought, "No wonder she hates me. I am so ugly."

She stood there with the scissors looking so accomplished, like she had just won a gold medal at the Olympics. I sobbed in the mirror and prayed silently that God—if there were one—would please save my sisters and me from this woman. Take us away. Wake us up from this. I would do anything for us to be safe, with food and clothes and parents who never hurt us. I felt repulsive.

She did this to the three of us quite often, cutting our bangs so short we looked like idiots. She played mental games with us until we were so drained that we had no energy to even participate. We became nothing. Nobodies. We became scared of both her and our father.

It was closer to the beginning of the two years when one day Diane insisted we go out to the backyard and each grab a stick. I think my sisters and I knew what she had planned, but we didn't want to believe it was about to happen. I sobbed as I walked back terrified and nauseated into the house with the stick Diane was about to whip me with. We each bent over per her demands, and she slashed the back of our legs and behinds with the very sticks we chose for her. She whipped us with those sticks until we were completely lacerated and raw. We cried and screamed and begged her to stop, but she continued, blow after blow. Each whip felt like there was a line of gasoline on my legs being lit on fire. I remember pulling my pants up in utter shame and embarrassment. I didn't care how bad it hurt. I didn't care that I had to walk funny to avoid the pain. I cared that I—that we—did not do anything to deserve this. We didn't deserve this life. We weren't terrible children who made trouble every chance we got. We tried not to smile or laugh, to talk to each other or even make weird looks that might aggravate her. Yet she still had it out for us. She still made it her sole purpose to harm us in the worst ways possible.

It was one of the worst days there, despite it being so close to the beginning of our time with our father and her, because we still had *some* dignity left. But after we pulled our pants up in pain, confusion, frustration, and humiliation, any dignity we had left quickly vanished into the thick and soiled air surrounding that putrid woman and the smirk on her face.

It wasn't long before Diane began to demand we complete a long list of household tasks, no matter how absurd it was to have little children do this. We had to wash carpet, scrub tiles, even scrape paint off windows and old wood. She loved to have us clean the bathroom with awful hazardous chemicals. For one whole week, we spent every hour after school stripping the paint off the cupboards in the kitchen. We had to use rags to put this orange stuff on them before we went to bed. When we woke up, we had to spend hours scraping the old paint off. We were all so tired at the end of the day. We didn't dare make a peep to complain about it because we were just so afraid of her.

In the beginning, my sisters and I desperately tried to make us work as a family. I think that is why we started lying about the abuse in the first place. Although their "discipline" was brutal and difficult to suffer, we did it anyway and never made a peep about it. I remember thinking that if I told the social workers some of the things that were going on they would take us away. I was afraid, first of all, of going back into foster care and, second of all, my sisters would never forgive me. After I realized they were doing the same, we silently agreed never to speak about the severe abuse we were enduring at home. I also think I secretly wished that by not telling anyone about the abuse, it would eventually stop.

During the first few months we were allowed to go outside for a few hours. We never had toys or games to play with (the day social workers came, toys were conveniently scattered throughout the house), so we made up our own. I usually plopped down on the ground and looked up the sky and dreamed about heaven. I prayed that God would wake up and send us somewhere safe. I would lie back into the grass and look up to the clouds and shut my eyes before tears fell down my temples.

After a few moments I would sit up and pick these little white flowers that were scattered throughout the entire yard. I picked hundreds of them. I think they were weeds; but I didn't care, they were prettier than I would ever be. I made sure that every three that I snatched were similar in length. I just sat there next to a big oak tree and braided the stems into a crown. I would put the crown on my head and dance around the backyard pretending to be the prettiest, most-spoiled little girl in the world. I pretended that I was a beautiful princess about to eat candy and fast food until my belly was so full I could barely move. I remember making flower crowns all the time. Sometimes, I made them for my sisters. I would wear the crown proudly until Diane screamed at us to come inside. Back to reality and this hellhole we were just beginning to learn to survive.

In the front of the house stood five enormous pine trees. One day my sisters and I stretched out on the grass and dreamed about tree houses and huge forts. We pretended we were the Swiss Family Robinson and lived up there. We dreamed of little houses placed throughout the trees. My sisters and I took turns, each describing our fantasy home. I remember I wanted my house to be pink with a bridge that went to every other house in the trees. We talked about elevators and big feasts and how, if dad or Diane ever came to the fort, we would throw rocks at them. Those houses meant we were safe from any harm. That was such a novel thought, a life where we were safe, well-fed, and knew that our parents loved us. I remember lying there and beginning to cry. I just prayed and wished that maybe the first couple of months in this house were just a terrible nightmare. "Please help my sisters and me, God. I promise I'll be a good girl," I thought. I really wished I lived in those trees. We even contemplated going back to our mother. At least there, no one hit us. Any life would have been better than this.

Diane's list of rigorous chores around the house grew longer and longer. As a seven-year old I knew it wasn't common to wake up and wash laundry and scrub a kitchen floor before school, but I didn't dare disobey. We worked around the house from the second we were ripped out of our beds in the morning until we had a break where we were at school, and then again until we drifted off to a very light sleep at night. We were scared, sore, and hungry. We barely ate anything, unless there were old leftovers or enough to make half peanut butter and jelly sandwiches.

After the chores became routine, Diane added a little twist. She wanted us to feel pain while we did our chores. She demanded that we stay in the bathroom while scrubbing it with toxic cleaning solvents. We were not allowed to come out until the bathroom was spotless.

She would run the water to wash dishes until it was scalding, much too hot for our hands, but she gave us no choice. Then, because we were slow, we were punished with a beating or a whipping with the infamous black belt. She would make us scrub the floor twice—maybe even three times after claiming to see a spot we missed. That was the thing with Diane; everything was psychological to her. It grew to be outrageous. She would claim to see things or smell something or, most infamously, hear things. She always claimed she could hear us talking about her or laughing. You think we had anything to laugh about? She wanted to be under our skin. She wanted to be superior to us. She beat us for hours on end and starved us for days at a time. The abuse had now grown from severely emotional to full-blown and grave physical, with long days without food and endless hours of torture.

As a seven-year-old, I began to wonder if maybe this was all part of growing up. I thought, I know grown-ups all have to do chores. Perhaps this was just the normal way to learn them. I thought, maybe all the other kids at school were suffering the same way we were. But in reality, this was not the case, and it didn't take long for me to see the difference. Our classmates were happy, healthy, well-dressed, and well-fed. They were children with dreams and hope. They had parents who loved them and protected them. I was so jealous.

Diane had an ulterior motive. She got satisfaction out of physically and mentally abusing us. With my experience living in so many foster homes, I had come to learn how to clean and do chores, but I did not know how to avoid vast amounts of pain while doing them Diane's way. My sisters and I would go to bed with knees raw from the kitchen floor. Our hands would be red and swollen from the dishwater. We would blow on them all night long. Camai and I, who shared a room, would sometimes take turns blowing on each other's hands quietly on the bad days. Poor Fawna slept in her own room and had to nurse herself. Our lungs were burned from the cleaning solvents and sometimes it was hard to breathe. I learned that if the solvents really got to me, taking short, shallow breaths helped bring less aggravation to my blistered throat.

After we nurtured ourselves the best we could, we would slowly drift off to sleep but never deep enough to not be prepared for some possible sick-minded event in the middle of the night. Sleeping on the top bunk, I was terrified of being snatched out during the early hours of the morning and smashed to the floor a half-second after becoming conscious. As Diane did that on occasion, it brought a scream out of me followed by a beating that was always hard to bear.

Diane began to make everything a game. How long can I throw this little girl around the house before she is lifeless? How long can I starve this girl until she begs for or steals food? Let's get this girl out of the shower while she is covered in soap and watch her squirm in irritation. We would scratch all night and morning only to find Diane smirking at us, giggling beneath her breath about how amusing it was to watch us scratch on our irritated skin.

One night Cam was instructed to take her shower. Diane had just bought hair dye and left the container in the shower. Camai thought it was shampoo and picked it up to use it and accidentally squirted some on the wall. She had no time to clean it up when Diane came storming in, telling her that her that her three minutes of showering was up. She ripped the shower curtain open to find the hair dye dripping down the shower wall.

Diane snatched Cam out of the tub and threw her to the floor. Diane kicked her and punched her and continued to bash her around the house as she dripped cold and wet. This was one of the first nights I began to feel a different kind of pain. It was not simply physical or mental. It was the pain that I could not protect my sisters. I would have given my own life for them at any time to stop that woman from hurting them.

As Cam sobbed in the bottom bunk, I began to weep in the top. I just begged God for some sort of mercy to get us out of this prison. I wanted him to help me protect my sisters and keep them safe. But by this time, God was invisible.

Diane had finally convinced us that we were bad kids. She constantly told us that there are jails for kids and we would be in one if it weren't for her and our father. She had succeeded in breaking everything she could. She finally forced us to believe that nobody would want us even if we were to be so lucky to move away. That was another one of the reasons that we continued to lie about being abused. We thought that if we were taken away, we wouldn't have anywhere to live. Even if someone were smart enough to believe us, nobody would ever want such ugly, bad kids. We never did anything really bad, though. We just minded our business every day, did our chores and tried to stay out of her way.

When we weren't doing chores or being beaten, we took turns sitting on The Green Chair in the kitchen. The upholstery was a sage-green vinyl material, the kind that your legs stick to when it's hot. My sisters and I had to sit there for hours at a time, hanging our heads. We had certain days assigned to each of us. I found it easiest to sit on my hands. That way my butt wouldn't get as sore so fast. If Diane ever caught me readjusting she would come up to me and squeeze me or yank my hair and scowl at me to stop moving, or she'd give me a reason to stop moving.

I never did like that chair. It was right next to the phone. I hated when the phone rang. That meant she would get up and answer it. I would just hang my head lower than usual and pray to God that she didn't have the energy to beat me at the moment that she finished her conversation.

My sisters and I were terrified of Diane. We would flinch every time she moved, even if she was on the other side of the house. We just took whatever we had coming to us; there was never any fighting back. We could scream and cry and tense our muscles up all we wanted, but we would never, under any circumstances, try to defend or even protect ourselves. Something like that would have been a miracle. But my sisters and I didn't believe in miracles.

Hungry—and Worse

Things started to get really bad at home. We were hardly allowed to go outside anymore. It seemed Diane thought that was too much of a risk. We couldn't dare let a neighbor or passerby see us because we might still have a small ounce of courage left to seek help. Even when we did go outside it was too hot with our sweaters and too cold with no jackets. We were only allowed to be less than a few feet away from the house in order to hear Diane's yell to summon us at any moment. There was a large mulberry tree in the backyard that stained our clothing when the berries fell off the tree on us. We learned quickly how important it was to not get stains.

If we were so lucky to play outside my sisters and I would pretend we were princesses living in a castle where we didn't need to do chores and Diane and dad didn't hurt us. It seems pretending, dreaming, and praying were the best ways to get through the worst days. If I could escape the terrors and pain for even just a few moments, it helped. So we would twirl around like other girls our age did and sometimes giggle from the thought of make-believe happiness. If Diane caught us cracking a smile, she made sure we had nothing to smile about. Bad kids are not allowed to smile. So going outside would be something of a getaway even if it were only a half hour in the rain or snow. Most of the time, though, we weren't allowed to go outside. That privilege was only for good kids.

Diane fed us on her good days. If we were really lucky we got a bowl of puffed wheat for breakfast, but we had two minutes to eat it. We hated puffed wheat. It was like eating a fluffy plant. Some days, it was the only thing we ate all day. Dad and Diane would buy it in those big plastic bags. This was probably because it was cheaper and had absolutely no sugar in it. Bad kids aren't allowed to have sugary cereal for breakfast. Sometimes if the store was out of puffed wheat, Dad and Diane were forced to get us puffed rice. It was a little better but still lacked sugar, and we still had only two minutes to scarf it down. I would eat as fast as I could, not caring what I looked like or that milk was going everywhere. "No wonder your dad doesn't love you; you eat like a little pig," Diane would scowl.

By this time, school had begun and was a little bit of a help to us. Not only could we go seven hours without any physical abuse, sometimes we had access to food through pizza parties or ice cream socials.

My sisters and I walked to school every morning by ourselves. Fawna became friends with a classmate whose house was on the way to school. It was black and white with a big screened-in porch that I loved to sit in while we waited. We would stop there sometimes if we weren't running late. She always offered us orange juice or a pop-tart. One day Diane must have figured out we had found another source of food. I think she followed us to school. She must have seen us stop there and me gobbling up the feast on the way down the porch. Diane had a belt and a whole list of chores waiting for us when we got home.

The Christmas holidays came and were anything but a joy to our world. I'll never forget these Christmas lights that my father had strung up in my room. He was really creative and spelled out a word with the lights, Noel. The lights were the only thing on in my room while I just sat there in the dark hoping for a scrap of food or to go to bed without a beating that night. They were red, green, blue, yellow, purple, and beautiful. I thought about how those lights represented Christmastime, and how we didn't celebrate Christmas. My sisters and I didn't get any presents. Diane took them away from us. One day in school we learned that Noel means peace. I thought it was ironic because I realized peace was probably what we had the least of in our home. I hated those lights when I got home that night. They were a lie.

Dad and Diane would rarely feed us dinner. We were always doing chores or sitting on The Green Chair. Sometimes we were sent to our rooms where we had to sit on our beds and not make a sound. They ate together every night, usually steaks or lasagna or some pasta dish that made my nostrils flare and stomach rumble like thunder when I smelled it as I sat in darkness. All three of us, whatever we were doing, stopped for a moment to wipe away tears from our cheeks. We were always so hungry. We wanted to eat at the dinner table like a normal family. Instead we were washing the basement walls with ammonia or scalding our hands on dishwater while they laughed and gobbled up their big, tasty dinners.

I think Diane told our dad that she fed us dinner before he got home. Either that or he had no heart in knowing we weren't eating dinner. He was never on our side. He didn't care about our safety or happiness because he wanted to marry Diane and, according to her, we were terrible kids who lied and stole and never listened to her simple requests. The balance of my father trying to have a loving relationship with his children and satisfying the love of his life had now completely shifted to her favor. His looks of disappointment and being ashamed were now the only emotions he ever expressed.

The days of loneliness, hunger, and no hope seemed to become unending. We had nobody to turn to. In the beginning we were allowed to have supervised visits with our mother, but my father and Diane told the social workers it would be best if we didn't attend these visits anymore. They had decided that the visits were too traumatizing for us. What a lie. Would we have told the social worker or our mother what was happening? I don't know what I would have said to him or her, or if I would have told anyone about what was going on, but at least I would have had the opportunity. We were too scared to tell people about the abuse, now thinking that if we did, those people wouldn't believe us. Not to mention if Diane were to find out, we would be trapped in her house standing in the face of death when we came back. Because we *always* came back.

At school I did my best to pretend that I was a normal kid. I tried to block out what my fate entailed after school each day. We all remained focused on our schoolwork, trying not to draw attention to ourselves. Diane would allow us to do homework. If she didn't, the teacher would call or send a note home and stir up all this commotion, setting up parent conferences or making frequent phone calls home. Diane was smart in letting us do our homework because that meant more time for her to have her way with us instead of dealing with teachers and the principal.

I took the homework privilege to my advantage. I would pretend that I had more homework than I really did so I could spend an extra hour or two at the kitchen table instead of getting beaten or doing painful chores. I even asked the teacher every day if she could give me extra spelling tests and worksheets to complete. I remember on Valentine's Day, I told Diane I had to write a page of compliments for each person in my class along with making them an individual Valentine each. That night I managed to do "homework" until bedtime. It was a really good night for me. But usually if one of us had a good night, it meant a not-so-good night for another one of us.

I vividly remember that night as I sat at the kitchen table and wept while I pretended to write compliments about my pupils and tried to block out the screaming and begs for mercy from my sisters. It was that instance when I realized we needed to start sticking together. The more homework I claimed to have, the more beatings my sisters would get that night. I had to start helping them out in any way I could. And they began to learn the same.

At school I was always hungry. I finally learned to time it so that I would get to school just in time for all the lunchboxes to be outside the classroom but not be late. It was a perfect plan. I would unzip a lunchbox full of heaven. There were sandwiches, chips, fruit, and candy in every pail. I usually grabbed three items, depending on how hungry I was, and stuffed them in my bag and walked into class. This was effective for a long period of time, until kids started realizing they didn't have the Snickers bar or apple in their lunchbox like their moms said were placed in there. I ate pretty well for a few months. Eventually, a letter was sent home and the lunchboxes got moved to a closet in the classroom. There went my only source of food for days at a time.

Diane assumed after reading the school letter that I was the kid taking things from the lunchboxes. When I came home that afternoon she forced me to drink liquid soap. I begged and pleaded with her not to make me do it. She took a spoon and shoved it down my throat. I began to gag and spit up a little bit. My throat felt like it was on fire. My eyes watered and snot poured from my nose. She explained that this should cure my hunger nicely.

Cam was also hungry all the time. At night I heard her stomach growling so loudly that it kept me awake. Her stomach just screamed for a little bite of something, anything. She never figured out the lunchbox thing like I did, so she had an empty stomach most of the day.

One night Cam gathered the courage to wake up once and raid the refrigerator. She tiptoed into the kitchen and grabbed whatever she could before Diane's hawk ears heard something and woke up. She never got away with anything good like cake or pizza; more like ketchup or moldy cheese. Cam did this a couple of times before Diane started noticing things in the refrigerator had been moved around or a little bit was missing out of a container. She rearranged the food items so that you had to move a lot of things around in order to grab something.

One night when the grumbling was really bad Camai tiptoed into the kitchen and slowly opened the fridge. She was very disappointed after finding everything was sealed into place. She had to move the gallon jugs and liters of pop in order to get something to take. The only thing in sight was the butter. It was on a little butter dish covered in plastic wrap. She didn't care. It was food to her. It was food to me, too.

She brought it back into our room and gobbled it up. I was already asleep, but I found out about her little triumph in the morning. Cam put the butter dish back just the way it was and Diane didn't even wake up. But her otherwise empty stomach must have been so upset with a belly full of butter. At least it was something, more than I was probably going to eat for that whole day. Camai was so happy she got to eat, and I was so jealous. But I was happy she got *something*.

Somehow, Diane figured the whole thing out. She dragged Camai out of her bed by her feet and I heard Cam's tailbone smash onto the floor. She pleaded for Diane not to hurt her, especially because her stomach was so upset. But Diane had no compassion. She had no heart and the blood running through her veins was cold. Ice cold.

Diane beat Camai until she couldn't even cry for mercy anymore. Cam practically crawled back into our room with scratches covering her face and bruises covering her body. She was bleeding a little bit, but all she cared about was not throwing up. Diane told her she was "a sick and disgusting pig" and that she looked like one, too. How dare you call my sister that. I was angered. Infuriated. Emotions of rage soon sped through my body. I think to myself, "You think that if a child sneaks into the kitchen in the middle of the night to eat butter that she's the pig? Look in the mirror, lady. You abuse, neglect, and torture three helpless, lifeless girls who did nothing to you. God, I hate you. Just let me die and take my sisters with me.

Soon after incidents like those I just lost all hope. I stopped caring about our schoolwork and life altogether. How can a child have a care for anything in the world when she is just fighting to survive? We took whatever Diane wanted to give us. She yelled at us every minute she had the chance and bashed us around every corner of the house. There were a couple of instances where things got unimaginably out of control. We saw no light at the end of the tunnel.

During the spring, Dad and Diane decided to have a garage sale. They sold most of our stuffed animals and the toys that we moved in with. We hardly even played with our toys at all. They sold a lot of my dad's exercise equipment and were also attempting to sell a bench press. Nobody was buying it, so at the end of the day Dad and Diane decided to just give it away. We were all sitting on the floor in the living room when Diane was making a sign that said FREE. My sisters and I began to giggle when she started walking outside with the sign and the bench press because we just thought it was comical that they had to *give* this thing away.

Diane set her stuff down except for a metal bar and told Fawna and me to return to our rooms. She had rage in her eyes. Her skin was dryer than ever, and I could smell the coffee on her breath even before she opened her mouth.

Diane started screaming at Camai. I was so scared for her. Cam stood in the living room and I could see it in her eyes, begging me not to leave her. But I had to. There was no way I could fight Diane. She was now screaming louder at Cam. I knew she wouldn't come in our bedroom, so I crept up to the door and peered through the crack.

Diane was circling Camai, yelling about her she had been getting on her nerves lately. Cam stood there sobbing while she pleaded for Diane not to hurt her. Diane never cared. We could have been on our knees begging for mercy, for our lives, for her to just leave us alone that one time, and she would not have cared one bit. She was a monster.

Diane took the metal bar and poked Camai in the stomach with it. Cam didn't budge. I saw a tear fall to the carpet as Cam's face remained emotionless. I felt terrified. I wanted to vomit, scream, and die all at once. Please let her live through whatever Diane is about to do.

Out of nowhere Diane lifted the massive hunk of metal and slammed it against Camai's head. I heard the cling against her skull. Her eyes rolled back into her head and she collapsed to the floor.

Diane dropped the metal bar and walked away.

I covered my mouth the moment it happened to muffle the scream. I started to cry hysterically. I sat down on my bed and prayed. I had stopped believing in God, but I still prayed anyways. I rocked back and forth and prayed as hard as I could. I didn't care if we stayed in this hellhole until the day we died. I just wanted my twin sister to be alive. I must have mouthed the words, "Please let her live," a thousand times.

I rocked back and forth for hours. When I heard Diane go downstairs into the basement, I scurried to the crack again. Cam was still lying there. I wanted to run up to her and shake her and have her just wake up and be okay. She continued to lie there, her face sticky from old tears.

I would guess about three hours had passed. I heard some mumbling outside my room. I knew Diane was standing there so I didn't dare get up. The sun was setting, and my room was getting darker every minute. I hated the nighttime. We had to sit, staring into the darkness, just waiting for our next rendezvous with her. It had been warm that day but as darkness fell I felt colder and colder. I wondered if this would be the day Fawna and I got to leave because Cam had been murdered. I pictured her lying on the shaggy carpet, lifeless. I pictured the police coming in and taking her body away in a body bag. All I could think about is how much I loved her and how I wanted to be dead because I couldn't imagine living this life without her by my side. Then I thought, if Cam were dead, Diane would surely kill us too.

I could hear my dad was home. I still didn't know if Camai was alive or not. At this point, I didn't care. If my twin sister were dead, I wanted to be too. I changed into some pajamas very quietly and crawled into my bed. I just prayed for hours that she was alive. I would have done anything to save her.

Sometime in the middle of the night our door quietly crept open. I heard the creak and knew by her soft entry it was she. I slept on the top bunk so I couldn't see her face. I then sat straight up to make sure it wasn't Diane with a knife. Cam walked slowly to the lower bunk and quietly crawled under the sheets. She didn't even change, just got right into her bed. Moments later, I heard her sobbing. I rolled over and hung my head over the side. "Cam?" I whispered.

"Yeah…what?" She replied quietly.

"Are you okay? You were lying there for a long time. You looked like you were dead," I whispered.

"I don't remember it," she replied. "I think I'm fine. I just have a really big bump on my head that I can't touch."

I told her I loved her and rolled back over and let out a big sigh. I was so relieved she was okay. I thanked God for letting her live that night, even though if she had died she would have been in a much happier place than here. Maybe God should have just let her die, so she could go dance in heaven and eat, and sleep, and never be hurt again.

During these nightmarish incidents, "we sisters" were all we had. Our prayers were what kept each other alive. Knowing that at the end of the day, we could look each other in the eye and feel support was what kept us going. I believe that's why God kept her alive that night, because we were all that each other had. To lose each other, we would have lost everything.

As if life were not at an all-time low, Diane started to become even *more* violent. She was in this phase where she would bash us around for hours, make us do some of her horror chores, and then throw us around some more. She would pull our hair out, chunks at a time. She would hit us, punch us, even kick us until we couldn't breathe. We would be lying on the floor as bloody pulps when we would turn around and she would tell us to go finish our duties. It soon became evident that her own issues were too much for her to handle, and she seemed to like taking them out on us.

My dad worked a lot. He left really early in the morning and came home late at night. When he came home, Diane would skip up to him the moment he opened the door and tell him what bad kids we had been that day. She would go on about how we acted out, how we yelled at her and didn't do any of our chores, and how she had to do everything herself because we refused. And then he would spank us and beat us even more.

My father and her had now completely brainwashed us. They put down all the people in our family, as the rambled on saying nobody loved us. Diane really liked to tear down our mother. She would tell us she was white trash and never loved us. She took the gift that I made for my mother for Mother's Day and smashed it against a wall. She told us that if the people in our family really loved us they would have come and taken us away by now. She told us all the time she spoke with our aunts and uncles, even cousins, and nobody wanted to even know us anymore. It was because our family didn't want to see such bad and ugly girls.

Sadly, I grew to believe her. I became convinced that we were going to die in that house. I truly believed that if we died, all of those people that we once shared our great memories with wouldn't even care. I figured she'd kill us, bury us in the backyard of that house in Brighton, and nobody in this world would even want to know.

Our lives were getting to a point where it was a struggle to stay alive. The mental abuse had become out of control. Diane insulted us as much as she could. She told us we were so ugly it made her throw up. She told us our own father couldn't even lay his eyes on us. The daily beatings and whippings became hourly beatings and whippings. One of the three of us was begging for mercy at all times during the day. We all took turns being the punching bag.

Because my dad enjoyed cooking, he whipped up great dinners for Diane and himself a few times a week. One day, my dad wanted to make something with chives. He heard about this place in Ohio that had fresh chives growing freely. We all piled into the car and drove to Ohio. It took about over an hour to get there. It was a hot and humid day. My father and Diane smoked so the windows were rolled down. I remember we were very hot and hungry this particular day.

When we got there we were allowed to get out of the car, only to help them look for this plant, but we had no idea what it looked like. My sisters and I ran through this field in the middle of nowhere. I felt like a wild child.

My sisters and I took off on our own routes. We ran around and hid in the tall cornfields nearby. I wanted to plop down in the field and stay there forever. I heard the stalks brushing around me and could tell one of my sisters was near. It was a few short moments of serenity, and I had never felt so calm. I got up and continued to run just because I could thinking Diane would never catch me. I couldn't see Ben and Diane, but I could hear their voices and a car in the distance. I thought we were the only people left in this world. The sound of the car grew louder and louder. I was lost and couldn't find my way out of the corn. All of a sudden I heard the car screech to a halt, and Cam let out a scream. Following the sounds, I was able to find my way out in no time.

Cam had run out of the corn into the road and was almost hit by this car. Dad and Diane dropped their plants and ran up to where Cam stood in the middle of the road. They waved to the driver with an apologetic look and directed Cam off to the side. The driver sped off, and Diane grabbed Cam's ear and started screaming in it. She told her that she was an idiot and a stupid girl. She slapped her and pushed her to the ground. Cam had begun to cry and looked scared to death.

Diane hauled Camai by her shirt to our car and threw her in the backseat. Cam cried hysterically. I had never seen her cry like that. I stood silently with my hands folded and head buckled to the tan gravel ground as the sun beat down on the top of my head.

We must have looked for those stupid chives for another hour while Cam sat in the car just baking. They didn't roll the windows down, either. I was sure she was so hot as I walked around only a few feet away from Diane.

When we returned to the car, I wanted to start crying. Cam was so sweaty. I could tell she had been crying the entire time. We all piled into the car and started on our way home. My father mentioned something about a smell, and Diane perked up with a devilish grin on her face. She turned around and said, "Yeah, she does smell like a fuckin' pig." She turned around and continued to laugh. Camai started crying again. I felt so bad. I squeezed her hand to let her know I loved her. I wanted to take Camai's pain away from her. It just wasn't fair. We didn't deserve this life.

Cam really took the abuse to heart. She sometimes wet the bed. It was her way of dealing with the stress. Most parents who have kids with a bed-wetting problem usually talk to the family doctor and form strategies to help their children stop. However, Diane had a different technique. Not only would she call Camai names—pig, filthy, disgusting slob, pathetic, every name in the book, she would punch her and slap her around in the middle of the night. When I was in bed and Diane stormed into our room I could see only the top of her head and her beating up my sister.

How could I watch that. That is my twin sister. One of t the only two people I love in this world. My only option left was to roll over and silently cry in my pillow, and hope she wouldn't come after me next.

If Diane came into our room in the middle of the night and smelled urine she would pull Camai out of bed by her hair. Cam would fall on the floor and of course begin to cry like any other eight-year-old girl would do. Diane would start to bash her around and scream at her. She would then pull her up to her feet by her ear and order her to strip the sheets off her bed and put them in the bathtub. Poor Cam. Three o'clock in the morning and this 8-year old little girl is washing her urine-soaked sheets in the bathtub by hand. She did all of this while Diane hovered over her screaming at her, telling her how disgusting she was for wetting the bed.

I don't know much about parenting or psychological issues with children, but I know enough to figure out that if a child is wetting the bed, responding with such a method won't solve the problem; it will only make it worse. And it did. So this bed-wetting and punishment turned into a vicious cycle in which Diane had complete control. She had complete control of everything. It didn't even matter anymore.

It appeared that my dad agreed with the abuse, at least the things he knew about. And how could he not have known more? You would think that if you came home and saw your children flinch at your every move, night after night, you might suspect something? Did he notice our little bodies were just skin and bone? How about all the bruises, burns, and bumps? Did he really think that we were such bad children that he needed to violently discipline us when he got home every night?

Once the summer came, my sisters and I were completely out of luck. School was our one hope, our escape from the hell we came home to. We ate at school and went half the day without getting beaten or screamed at. We knew we were in for it. It was all just a matter of time.

The summer days were long and hot. It seemed as if it was hotter in our house than it was outside. Our chores were never-ending, along with the beatings and the hunger. If we were lucky, Diane allowed us one peanut butter and jelly sandwich a day. Because school was out, she stayed home with us while our dad was at work all day. The yelling and hitting never stopped. Diane just got more violent and more severe with every day we were lucky enough to wake up to.

I remember one day in May. I was wearing a purple long-sleeve shirt and a pair of black spandex pants. I was sweating but continued to do all of my work. I was then ordered to sit in The Green Chair while my sisters did their chores, and then we switched. We did chores and had no lunch all day. Around four in the afternoon Diane ordered us to sit in different areas of the house. She said it was our punishment for not finishing our chores on time. I went to my room and sat on the bottom bunk.

I started thinking about the upcoming school year and the possibility that I would be able to make some friends. Maybe I could have my first best friend. Maybe Diane would start treating me better and let me have sleepovers and be in the Girl Scouts. One time in the beginning she did let me go to the movies with some girls in my class. I thought that maybe if I made some friends in the next school year that she'd let me do that again. I would have done anything for Diane to just like me. For her to not think I was ugly. I snapped back to reality when I heard her shuffle on the other side of the house.

I heard Diane stomp all the way to my room. I froze up and snapped my head down. I put my hands under my butt in the position we are supposed to sit. Diane smashed the door open and stormed in. She never looked so terrible. Her red hair was faded, frizzy and frayed. The dry skin on the edges of her nose was flaking off. Her teeth were stained from all the coffee and her breath reeked of it. For a second I thought back to those times when she used to seem so beautiful—inside and out. I imagined those days when Diane used to smell like flowers and her smile sparkled so big. I wanted nothing more than to go back to those happy times.

Her appearance was frightful. I quickly transitioned to self-defense mode. I became concerned with nothing but protecting myself and tensed up as best I could. She began screaming about something I had done wrong. I was scared but there was nothing I could do to stop her.

Tears flushed down my cheeks. My stomach churned and my heart began to thump fast. This was always my first reaction. Her breath was rancid and her brown eyes surged with pure rage. I leaned back towards the bed but she just inched closer over top of me. She began thrashing me around the bed. My body tensed up more. She got really close to my face and continued to scream and threaten me.

She grabbed my arms to get even closer to my face and then let go to smack me. She squeezed my arms even tighter and then pushed my face down into the bed where it became submerged in the bedspread and pillow. Soon I couldn't breathe. My first thought—and what I thought would be my last thought—was that she was going to suffocate me this very moment. I thought, "Just kill me. I don't even want to live anymore." My mind flashed with thoughts about how bad my sisters would get it if I died. I said a quick prayer for their safety and started yelping as loud as I could. I grunted and screamed words that were sometimes clear and sometimes muffled by the scratchy comforter. She bellowed: "Think you're so cute, don't you! You always try to act like the sweet one! Well, how cute do you think you look now, you ugly little brat!"

Then she bashed my head around like a kid playing with a ball. I could feel snot and saliva covering my face and soon stopped trying to protect myself. My body soon went limp, and before I knew it I felt something really hard hit the back of my head. She pushed my head back down to the bed and grabbed my hair to pull me back up. I was crying and begging her to stop.

All of a sudden, out of nowhere, she completely relaxed her grip from my head and let me fall back to the bed. Her face turned white as a ghost and her eyes dilated from a state of anger and rage to complete distress.

She politely asked me to stand up and put my hand on the back of my head.

I felt something really warm and sticky and my hair was soaked with it. I was trying to figure out what it was but I began to feel lightheaded and extremely dizzy. My knees started to give out and my body felt like it was going to collapse.

Diane put her arms around me to help me walk and said in a soft voice, "Whatever you do, do not move your hand."

What the hell? Why is she talking to me like that? What has she done? I was in complete confusion.

I continue to feel the very warm liquid drip through my fingers, trickle down my arm and down my neck. I felt like I wanted to go to sleep, but Diane was nudging me toward the bathroom. I was so confused about what had happened and why she was treating me with this very unusual maternal instinct.

When we got to the bathroom she turned the light on and had me kneel down over the bathtub. I hung my head over the tub and began to feel nauseous with the smell of fresh Clorox. Diane told me

I could let go of my hand, so I slowly moved it off my head and rested it on the side of the tub. Diane rolled up a towel and wrapped it around the back of my head and applied pressure. I was so dizzy and I couldn't understand what was going on. I knew I was hurt, probably pretty badly if Diane was treating me this way. I just wanted to see my sisters. I wanted them to tell me I would be okay. I started to cry silently as my tears dripped into the puddle of blood now forming in the bottom of the tub.

Diane yelled for one of my sisters to go get her more towels but then decided she didn't want to stain them. She told me to crawl inside the tub and lie down until she figured out what to do. She told me to close my eyes and try to fall asleep. I did as she said. After what seemed like two minutes I opened my eyes. My body felt warm but stiff and damp as I shivered from a cold draft whisking by.

I was lying in a bathtub now almost completely lined with my deep red blood. It was the warmest near my head, so I put my hand back there and yelped in pain as I touched the wound. My pants and shirt especially were soaked in blood and my hand was covered with dried blood that was stuck in my fingernails and the dry cracks of my hand.

I got really scared and started to panic. I tried to sit up but felt like as I moved I was going to pass out. Diane must have heard me scuffling around. She slowly walked into the bathroom and instructed me to sit up and time for me to clean up. Her face was emotionless; her eyes were empty.

She turned the water on and told me to make sure all of the blood was gone. I climbed out of the tub slowly and put my head over the side again. I looked out the window and it seemed to be getting dark outside. I knew my dad would be home soon. I wanted him to come home and find his daughter lying in a bathtub bleeding to death. As I rinsed my own blood down the drain my head started to throb. I saw clots and a few chunks of hair trickle down the side of the tub and get stuck in the drain. There was blood everywhere.

I felt so disgusting but was in so much pain that I couldn't even care. I put my hand back there and felt an enormous bump. I wanted to pass out because of the pain. I felt blood start to gush out from the wound as soon as I touched it. I prayed that I would die. "She could never get rid of this blood fast enough before the police arrived," I thought to myself. Then everyone would know what a monster she was for abusing, and murdering, innocent children.

Diane had me get out and change into some dry clothes. She was going to make it look like nothing happened. She was going to try to cover it up before my dad got home. Blood dripped onto the tub out of my hair for what seemed like forever. Blood continued to drip so she had me lean over the tub again. There were a couple of bloody rags on the floor and some blood in the sink. It looked like someone was murdered in there. I began to feel achy and nausea now consumed me.

After a few minutes I heard a familiar voice. It was my dad. I heard his work boots clunk on the kitchen floor and hoped he would come in soon to take care of me. I heard Diane talking. It sounded like she was pleading with him. She was stuttering and rambling while telling him "her side" of the story.

My dad walked over to the bathroom and slowly leaned in the doorway. He was standing over the bathtub towering over me. By the way my head was hanging over the side of the tub I could see him upside down. He seemed emotionless, except for his now customary look of disappointment. I remember thinking that maybe he was really concerned and trying to be strong for me.

He just shook his head and turned away. He didn't even touch me. It was in this moment that I became assured my father was never again to be considered an ally. He just wanted to make Diane happy, and, if that meant ignoring your bleeding-to-death eight-year-old daughter, then so be it.

About an hour had passed when Diane came back in the bathroom and told me it was okay for me to stand up. I stood and she then guided me to my room. With her help, I crawled into my bed on the top bunk and laid down on my soft pillow. I had to sleep on my side because it hurt so bad to even put the least bit of pressure on the bump. Diane shut the light off. I wanted to go to sleep so badly but was afraid to. Diane told me she would check on me every hour but she didn't come into my room once. I started crying after she left as I tried to take care of my wound. I just thought to myself, "I can't believe she cracked my head open."

Cam quietly stood up out of her bunk bed and grabbed my arm. "You okay Jas?"

"I think so. The bitch cracked my head open." Cam stroked my arm for a few moments, which makes me feel somewhat at ease. I think, "If I die tonight, I would die happy knowing my sisters love and care about me, and Cam is right by my side."

When I awoke a few short hours later, I was in so much pain. My head was pounding. My hair was tangled and snarled and covered in dried blood. I looked around my room to find what she smashed my head into.

She didn't let me shower before sending me to school with no breakfast. She put my hair up using a rubber band to disguise the dried blood and massive gash on my head. In school that day I felt light-headed. Things were really blurry but I tried my best to remain focused because I didn't want to draw attention to myself. At school that day was an ice cream social that I had looked forward to for weeks—free ice cream.

I went to the bathroom during recess and spent a half hour trying to nurse my wound. I used the sink to clean up my head by cupping my hands and splashing water on my scalp and to rinse my hair. I used the hand soap and gently washed my scalp around the crack, which caused pure agony. I could feel a really big gash line with a lot of swelling on the edges. I spent all of recess trying to clean my head and hair, and when I walked out of the bathroom, I realized that I had missed the ice cream social. I went back into the bathroom and sat on the floor and just wept. This was just not fair.

The way that Diane treated us at home was at its worst. We were fed little food. She used every minute my father wasn't home to abuse us. She used us for labor around the house, things only adults should be doing. We were hit, punched, slapped, kicked, whipped—everything you can think of that would cause harm to a person. And the worst part about this whole thing was that there was nothing my sisters and I could do about it.

The Social Workers Come—and go

6

On the first day of third grade I walked into the classroom wearing a dirty and worn-out t-shirt that hid most of the scars and bruises residing on my frail body. I could hear my classmates snickering and wondering why I smelled like Clorox and old sweat.

I had no life in me. I had no energy, ambition, or desire to be there. My face was blank; my eyes were empty. At this point I had stopped thinking of school as a temporary escape. I didn't even care if I was at home being slapped during endless games or doing chores. It wouldn't have a made a difference. I was a little girl with no dreams and no love. I had one concern in life—making sure my sisters were alive at the end of the day. Whether that meant they were bleeding, sobbing, or begging for mercy, all I cared about was whether they were still breathing and still my sisters. They were the only reason I was still alive. They were the only reason I got up in the morning. They were the only purpose for making it through the long, grueling days.

Of course we had visits from the social workers who had put us into the mess. It was rare that any social worker stayed on our case for a long period of time. They would just come and go. Diane would be nice to us the day before their visit and turn back into her old self the second they walked out the door.

Social workers noted a few problems right off the bat. Diane's observed 'discipline' was termed "excessive or at least ill-advised." The worker at the time encouraged counseling services to not only address this issue but to also help shape us into a happy family. My father was quick to resist the offer as Diane convinced him counseling was not necessary. They noted my sisters and I were extremely desperate at first to create a cohesive family unit but expectations were unrealistic and there seemed to lack a desire for any form of love and acceptance on Diane's part. The caseworker at the time noted we were also due for dental and medical evaluations—a statement that would be reiterated eight times in the next two years.

Lastly, the social workers noted that there was a strong, unhealthy, superior relationship between Ben and Diane, and that anything my father did was subject to approval by Diane. They described her as controlling, rigid, and now hard to get along with. Caseworkers went as far to state that although they were happy when Ben stepped in for the first time in our lives, it appears he stepped up only to allow Diane to care for us.

They also did physical and mental examinations on us. Their conclusion: we were "troubled children." With Diane's lies combined with our inability to be honest, they noted in the files that we were devious kids and were lucky to have our father and Diane put up with us. We were further described as story-telling manipulative girls who desperately want a family but don't seem to want it bad enough. Their explanations further went on to allege that our apparent wounds and bruises were either self-inflicted or caused by typical childlike acts such as temper tantrums.

Diane would tell each of them an elaborate story about how bad we were. I think the social workers believed her, too. She would cry fake tears about how she would do anything just to be our mother but we just wouldn't accept her; that we were jealous of her, and acting out was our way of getting back at her. The social workers wrote all of this down and seemed to believe it in its entirety. They went on to write that we were kids who just wanted attention and made up stories with the sole purpose to become the center of it.

The fact was we did steal and we did lie, like the social workers noted. But nobody ever asked us the real reason why we stole (to eat) and lied (to protect ourselves and each other). Of course nobody would want us. The social workers knew that they could never pawn us off on another foster family. All they could think about was how much paperwork and headaches would be caused by putting us back into foster care. So Diane would go on and tell them that she would try harder to form a bond with us, and also work with us to have a better relationship. Diane was satisfying the socials workers by suggesting she would make greater efforts for the sake of our "family" and the social workers were in return satisfying Diane by letting us stay with my father and her. Month after month, visit after visit, this cycle continued. There really was no way out.

Since Diane constantly hammered into our minds that nobody would want us if we were taken away, we finally grew to believe her—especially considering how the social workers treated us during their visits and how they continued to leave time after time without taking us with them. Diane would say she read the reports from the social workers and we were so lucky to not be put back with that "excuse for a mother" we had. She really hated my mother. This was just another way of hurting us, tearing down my mother who my sisters and I wanted to believe so badly would get her act together and fight for us someday.

We became convinced we were bad kids. We believed that we deserved any punishment and discipline that came our way. Our lives had arrived at a point where nothing mattered. We stopped praying to God. We stopped pretending to be happy in school. We had completely given up.

During one long afternoon of Diane bashing us around the house, she kept repeating "just wait until your dad gets home." She was talking about how we were really going to get it and that we would learn a lesson about being disrespectful. Hearing those words were terrifying. He had begun to get involved in some of the physical violence and we hadn't yet experienced his full potential yet. That day, I remember, I was more scared of my father than of her. I just knew that night would be bad.

He finally came home from work after what seemed like an eternity. It was dark.

They went into their room for about 20 minutes. He seemed really fed up, as if he was just sick and tired of this life they had created. I could hear him and Diane in the other room fighting. They had started to do this quite often. He kept saying things about how we should just go back into foster care because she obviously didn't want us. They continued to bicker and the fight escalated to shouting. I heard their bedroom door slam open and after a few silent moments Cam was called into the kitchen.

Cam and I were sitting together in our bedroom. We sat close on the bed and I squeezed her hand. I felt a pit in my stomach as she got up quickly but slowly looked back at me with tears in her eyes.

"I'll be okay Jas, be strong." Her voice cracked as she attempted to comfort me despite knowing her fate.

I sat with a half-smile trying to reassure her back that I knew she would be okay. Tears fell like rain down my cheeks and I quickly brushed them away so she could see *I* was the one being brave for *her*.

Fawna had been seated on The Green Chair during all of this. I could hear the rage and frustration in my fathers voice as he yelled again, louder, for Cam. He started yelling at her. I could just picture him in her face as she looked at the ground. I heard some commotion but just put my head down and stared at the carpet. I covered my ears with my hands and started to dream about those castles where little girls are never hurt.

Diane had informed my father that Cam had been "talking back." He picked her up and dropped her on the counter next to the kitchen sink. He began to force her to swallow some dish soap he forcefully rammed into her mouth. She was crying and squirming. Fawna was sitting a mere six feet away. She hung her head and tried not flinch but the pain she felt at not being able to protect her little sister was unbearable.

My father scooted his hands under Cam's legs and picked her up and slammed her down on the hard countertop. He tried again to get her to swallow the soap but when she sobbed and resisted he picked her up under her arms and slammed her a few more times on the counter. She sobbed louder and begged for him to stop. This cycle continued for about eight or nine times until my father became exhausted and let Cam crawl back to our room. Her legs and behind had been painfully smashed on the countertop as my precious sister cried and wailed and pleaded for mercy.

I couldn't believe how he pounded my sister on the countertop as she begged for the pain to stop. Cam limped into our room with tears streaming down her soft, flushed cheeks, with fresh bruises but an old, wounded heart. My own heart just ached for her. I held her in my arms and cried. How can God let this happen to us? What did we do to deserve this? That's when I heard my father's voice louder than ever.

Cam laid in my arms on the bottom bunk as I put my hand over her ear to protect her from what was about to happen to our sister. She didn't need to hear it.

We sat together on the bottom bunk as I rocked back and forth.

Be strong, Fawna. It will be over soon.

As Fawna had been sitting in the kitchen just a few feet away from our sister enduring severe physical pain, Diane was in the living room, just a few feet away from my room. Instead of watching my father beat his own little innocent girl, she sat there on the couch staring at Fawna on The Green Chair. Fawna knew she was being watched like prey by a predator.

She soon rose from the couch and got close in Fawna's face. She started screaming at her, "What, do you like it when your sister feels pain? You're sick that you like that! Ben, you see that? Your own daughter is so sick she likes punishment!"

My father quickly followed suit and got in Fawna's face too. He picked her up by the clothes on her chest and pinned her up against the wall next to The Green Chair. He screamed in Fawna's face about talking back to Diane and asked her if she was lying. I held Cam closer to me as he continued to scream, "Don't lie to me!"

Fawna wept and shouted, "I'm not lying, dad!"

He pushed her over to the door that had a glass window in the center. He grabbed a stronger hold of her clothes and lifted her off the ground to pin her higher against the glass. Fawna remembers the moment as losing the ability to breathe; my father's grasp on her pinned against the door was so strong he was pushing the very breath out of her little lungs. She felt as if her chest was going to cave in as his fists pushed harder and his voice grew louder with every scream. Diane stood just a few inches behind him with a gruesome smirk on her face.

Fawna began to see darkness. She felt like she was going to black out from the inability to breathe. She thought, "I'm going to die, right here, right now. He's going to suffocate me. I don't know if there is a God, but if there is one, please let me live. I love you sisters."

At that very moment she closed her eyes and felt oxygen fill her lungs and a rush of relief. My father had pushed her so hard the glass popped behind her and Fawna fell to the floor as little shards of glass rained around her sad, scared face. The glass was shattered and scattered around her as she quickly realized she was alive.

It was the first time Fawna was certain Diane had won. She won Daddy's heart, and we now fended for ourselves and our sisters. My father would never protect us.

My sisters and I continued to suffer insurmountable pain day in and day out. We had nobody to turn to. The other kids at school wouldn't dare be our friends and teachers and the principal just seemed to feel sorry for us. They called our social workers several occasions, but the social workers continued to write in our files that we were story-tellers and to blame for most of the turmoil.

I remember that in the beginning, I tried to communicate to the social workers somehow. I always tried sending them some kind of secret message. They sometimes talked with us in a room away from Dad and Diane. I always loved Diane's face when they did this. It was an "oh shit" kind of thing. It was if she was actually worried they might learn the truth. She would put on this act by being so nice right before the social worker took us into another room, saying sweetly, "It's okay honey, don't be afraid. Just tell them the truth. They won't be mad at you for being bad." Ha. In my eight-year-old mind I thought, "Okay Diane, you want me to tell them the truth? You would go to jail, you psycho no-hearted bitch."

Our file indicates that my sisters and I said at every visit that we wanted to continue living with my father and Diane. I wish I could have found the courage to ask them to take us far, far away. I wonder now if they would.

Sometimes my father would come home and not even talk to Diane before spanking us. It became a routine. He came in the door, hung up his heavy jacket and keys, came in our rooms and spanked each of us one by one. Diane seemed pleased she didn't have to beg for him to spank us anymore. As he walked towards me I saw her shadow in the background with that smile on her face. She was a sick woman.

His spankings hurt more than Diane's. His hands were bigger and had so much more force. I just wanted to be Daddy's little girl. My heart longed for my Dad to love me and not hurt me anymore. I would have done anything to just have him love me again. I just wished for a mom and a dad, a best friend, and sisters I could play with. Instead, we were fending for our lives and struggling to make it through each day.

Life as we knew it became a constant psychological battle. Choosing between finding food and protecting each other became a regular routine. Often we chose the latter. The feeling of being hungry developed into an overall numbness accompanied by a faint weakness but sharp pain. Our bodies screamed for food, but filling that void was not an option. If we were lucky enough to get scraps they were gobbled down like slop during a pig feeding. It wasn't pretty, but who cares—neither were we.

Soon fights between my father and stepmother began to occur every day. They would scream at each other until the late hours of the night. Often we heard pushing and shoving, screaming, and things breaking. Sometimes those fights were followed by psychotic tirades by Diane storming into our rooms, dragging us out of our beds by our hair and thrashing us around for an hour. We would cry and yelp as our exhausted, broken little bodies smashed up against walls and our faces collided with the hands of a putrid woman with a mission to murder us with no mercy. Now, for the first time, she was handing out violent abuse even when my father was there.

I remember asking myself, "Dad, aren't you home? Don't you hear us being kicked and whipped and beaten alive? Don't you hear our cries for help? We need you...." I soon realized my father was a weak. He had no self-worth as he listened to this monster he loved so much harm his innocent, helpless children. He had no right having us, ever.

Their tension soon grew to become our tension. Their disagreements surmounted to more violence by Diane onto us. The more they fought, the worse we had it. She was now trying so hard to convert my father back into the man who thought his children were bad. He was also feeling more pressure from the social workers to put the entire family under the treatment of a DHS-ordered psychiatrist and to use resources practically given to him for free to help our situation that the social workers now knew was anything but good. Our file was now indicating that corporal punishment seemed apparent and discussions with Ben and Diane regarding this serious matter were being held on a weekly basis. But, they continued to note we "weren't doing anything to help the situation" and still left us in the home after each visit. Records indicate social worker visits to the home around this time were now six or seven times per month rather than the normal one.

If we were lying, it was because we had to. If we stole, it was because we needed food. But the fact that my father knew we were crying out for help and didn't do anything to stop her makes him just as much of a criminal.

After Diane whipped me with the belt one day my bottom was so sore I could barely sit down. Bruises and welts crisscrossed my behind while tears emotionlessly fell down my face. When my father came home that night he immediately came into my room. A black belt hung in his left hand while his right hand rested on his hip. He looked drained but on a mission. I saw determination in his eyes but disappointment in his heart. His silhouette in my doorway made me quiver as terror shook my soul.

He turned the light on to expose me sitting, shaking and scared. He didn't speak a word as he sat down on my bed and motioned for me to bend over his lap. I walked so slowly over to him. I was already trembling and pleading to him with my eyes not to spank me. He put me over his legs and raised his arm. I began to squirm like a wild horse and begged him not to do it.

"No Dad, please Dad, don't! Please no! I will be a good girl! Please!" I pleaded. He paused for a quick moment. I don't know where the courage came to even ask for him to not whip me just this one time, but something deep inside of me caused me to yell out for help.

Diane stood in the hallway practically giggling. He looked confused while an uneasy smile appeared on his face in response to his wicked wife now full-out laughing at a helpless child's request to not be hurt this one time.

"I haven't even done it yet…. Why are you squirming?"

I looked up at him and felt hot on the inside. I was imploring with my eyes for him to just listen to me this one time.

He must have understood. For the first time he must have looked into my eyes and read my request for mercy. He told Diane to go get something. As I stared down at the carpet over his lap I pictured Diane skipping down the hallway with a big grin. He leaned his head down to me and in a soft but deep tone asked, "Is there something you need to tell me?"

"My butt…it just…already hurts… so much." I couldn't breathe fast enough between the words of my sentence. "Please…Dad." My nose was running everywhere and tears dripped like a faucet leaking onto the floor.

I knew in my heart he believed me. The only problem was he had another very important woman in his life he needed to make sure was satisfied.

He had me go into the bathroom and pull my pants down. I was absolutely humiliated. I was crying even more as I shamefully stood in the bathroom doorway with my pants around my ankles showing my bare butt to my own father so he wouldn't spank me for just this one night.

My father stood in the hallway with a blank face and his hand covering his mouth. He looked so superior and I could tell he was livid. I could see it in his face that he didn't want to believe someone could do this to his little girl.

He let out a long sigh. Diane came from the kitchen and started laughing hysterically as she rested her hand on my father's back. My face immediately turned bright red and disgrace filled my little body. She turned around and walked into the living room. My dad told me to pull my pants up and go back to my room. I stopped crying for a minute as I started to pray. "Thank you God, for giving me this one night. I just needed you this one night, God."

My dad followed me back to my room and sat down on the bed with me. Then he bent me over his lap. Another rush of tears consumed my face. I cried and wailed as he spanked me harder than ever before. I screamed and cried as loud as I could. As I flinched with each blow I pictured Diane sitting on the couch just a few feet away from this disgraceful scene. Rage filled my body as I took the last of it. Diane knew she had won. As soon as she hears the cries and the begging for mercy she knows she has won.

That kind of situation now happened all the time. In the end my father's last concern was that Diane was happy. Because if she was happy, he was happy. I know deep down he wanted us all to be a happy family but he knew it was never going to work. He knew from the beginning that Diane would always be in competition with his three little girls and he could never make her feel good enough. So, as long as he worked a lot, was nice to the social workers, and did whatever he needed to do to make Diane happy, everything was fine.

There were a few instances where I gained a glimmer of hope about someone finding out what was happening to us. One social worker who actually seemed on top of things came to our house one day and took each of us sisters separately into a room by ourselves. She asked us questions that nobody had asked us before. She asked us if Diane hurt us and if we would rather live somewhere else. She wrote a lot down on her notepad. She listened intently as I lied about each mark on my body. I think she could tell I was lying as she continued to pry about my physical appearance.

She even came back a few days later and did some more interviewing. When she did my physical examination she wanted me to explain every scar, bruise, bump, and welt on my body. I began to run out of lies for each bruise and scar so I began to tell her "I don't know" for every other mark on my body. She was a smart woman.

But she wasn't smart enough to take us away. I think Diane listened outside the door when I tried to secretly tell the woman to take us with her and never bring us back. Later that night Diane taught me a lesson that I'll never forget, and we never heard from that social worker again.

When it came to the abuse I tried to avoid the pain as much as possible. I learned to position body parts in certain ways in order to reduce injuries. For instance, when Diane kicked me I turned my legs or body to the side, which lessened the impact. When she slapped my face I turned my head away from her so I would have less sting from the smack. I felt like a ruler of the world when I won little battles like this. She had no idea I was defeating her in my own way.

But, Dawn had her own way of winning battles. One frigid morning in January began like usual. Like always, we woke up, did our chores, and set out on our walk to school. The cold was *really* cold. My whole body was numb. I couldn't even talk because the cold air hurt my throat. My sisters and I plodded on for the eight blocks to our elementary school. When we got there we found out it was closed. We were the only ones there. We were standing there with no winter jackets, no breakfast, and not a hope in the world. We returned home very slowly and sadly and walked in to find Diane laughing at us. She found it so funny that we walked to school in the freezing cold only to discover school was closed for the day. And she knew that school being closed meant a full day of beatings and torture.

Diane had two little lizards as pets. She brought them with her when we all moved in together. She kept them in a huge tank in the family room. Diane was obsessed with them. Every time we went to the grocery store she would buy them something to eat or play with or to make their tank more appealing. She cared more about those darn lizards than she did us.

One day she came home with a heated rock for them to sleep on. I couldn't help but think about how every night I shivered until I fell asleep and woke up absolutely frozen. I would have loved a heated rock to sleep on. I hated those lizards. They had a better life than me. They were fed, kept warm, and never, under any circumstances, harmed. I wished I was a lizard.

One day, for some reason, Cam was instructed to sit down at the kitchen table for lunch. Fawna and I were so angry because we were so hungry. As if it was this huge privilege to be given food. Cam slowly walked into the kitchen and sat down on the bench. There was an empty plate on the table with no silverware next to it. Diane had a weird smirk on her face and I could tell by her body language she had something sick up her sleeve.

She went into the family room and took out one of the lizards. She crept back into the kitchen with it crawling all over her hand and arm. She was smiling. She set it down on Camai's empty plate. Cam looked at it and tears welled up in her eyes. Diane thought it was hilarious. Cam was so hungry. We all were. Diane began to laugh and dance around the kitchen. She cackled a few more times and then proclaimed, "What's wrong, Camai, is this lizard not good enough for you? I offer you food and you don't even take it!" She was such a sick woman.

The fight for food went on and on. We tried to think of new ways to get food. When we went grocery shopping I always got something to eat. Of course it wasn't a typical little kid asking mommy for some fruit roll-ups or chips. I had to sneak something directly into my mouth. If we walked by the bulk candy display I pretended to have to tie my shoe, and I would pick up a gummy worm or jellybean from the floor and quickly shove it into my mouth. I placed it in between my teeth and the inside of my cheek so that I could save it for later and not give myself away by chewing it.

In the winter I was really in luck. While Diane checked out at the cash register we had to stand by the one-cent ponies. Big bags of road salt were always next to the ponies. My eyes lit up every time we walked into the store because I could always find a bag with a rip it in. I couldn't tie my shoe again because Diane would get suspicious, so I dragged my feet a certain way to push the spilled salt into a little pile. When Diane reached for the receipt or turned to walk out the door I would dip down and grab a handful of the road salt from the floor in a heartbeat. I actually got really good at doing this. I shoved the salt into anything—a pocket, a shoe, even my underwear—just to get it home.

When we got home I ate my treasure from the store. I nonchalantly placed one piece in my mouth at time, putting it in between my cheeks and teeth to make it last as long as possible. Mmmmm, road salt. It actually felt like a treat and kept me grumble-free for a couple of hours.

One time that we went to the store, it looked like the same bag was ripped open from our previous visit. The hole was so big that I just grabbed a handful right from the bag. I was set with enough food to last me for days.

I didn't really mind eating the salt. Sometimes I got some dirt in the mix as one would expect. Eventually, though, the salt began to burn my mouth. I used to get big sores on the inside of my mouth and tongue, and it felt like there were holes in the sides of my cheeks. Road salt is not meant to be eaten. But every time we went to the store in the winter I came home with dinner. I sucked on the pieces, one by one, until all of them were gone. When Diane came in my room or the kitchen to make sure I was behaving she had no idea I was devouring a little snack. Another battle—won.

After about a year and a half of nothing but puffed wheat for breakfast we got really sick of the plain taste. It's natural for kids at that age to want sugar or some kind of flavoring. We decided to get smart and add our own. As soon as Diane walked out of the kitchen in the morning Fawna would scoot her chair to the bottom cabinet next to the refrigerator and snatch the syrup bottle. She brought it back to the table and we took turns quietly pouring the syrup into our cereal bowls. I had to try so hard not to laugh. How great it was to feel victorious! The syrup didn't really taste good with the cereal but I didn't care. It tasted better than what we were given to eat, that is if it was anything at all.

Diane eventually found out about the syrup like she did everything else. She took the syrup away and hid it somewhere in the house. We were all beaten that night. We also weren't allowed to have our puffed wheat breakfasts for weeks.

At this point, Diane's game playing and bashing us around the house was old news. However, if she could think up something that involved both of those, she was in heaven. Her favorite involved getting us to hate our father.

Immediately after returning from school we were ordered to go to our rooms. She would have me sit in the middle of the floor while she leaned up against the dresser and crossed her arms with a devilish grin on her face. Her stance alone was enough to give me that bad feeling, the feeling we got when we knew it was going to be a long night.

She would stare me down and begin to circle me in hopes to intimidate me. I would start to cry and just hang in my head, looking between my crossed legs. Diane would start the cycle.

"Jasmine, why do you hate your dad?"

I would look up at her and reply quietly, "I don't hate my dad." I sniffled and choked on my tears as I started to become frustrated and filled with agony.

Diane would then walk up to me, and do whatever she was in the mood for—punch me, slap me upside my head, or kick me in the stomach. I would fall to the floor and lie there, just sobbing.

Once I regained the strength to sit up again, I would press my hands to the floor and prop myself up, my head still hanging low.

She would back up and get in the same position she started in.

"Jasmine, I'm going to ask you again, *why* do you hate your dad?"

I would again look up at her in sorrow and reply, "I don't hate him," or "I love my dad."

Then Diane would slap me or kick me, something different than what she did just before. This process would repeat for what seemed like hours until I finally gave up and told her I hated my father, just so I could escape the pain. After I claimed hatred for my own father, my stepmother would give me one final blow and walk out of the room with vindication and excitement.

The second my father came home she would run up to him gleaming as if she had just won the lottery, and exclaim, "Jasmine told me she hated you today, Ben!" My father would look at me and shake his head. One time tears even welled up in his eyes. I stopped being able to look him in his eyes because I just couldn't bear to see his reaction to this awful proclamation anymore. It just crushed me to think he actually believed her. I prayed that he never really did believe her, and that he would be upset that I had been forced to say those words under unimaginable circumstances.

I would have given anything to shout, "No Dad! I don't hate you! I love you! I had to say I hated you just so Diane would stop hurting me!" I could never do that, though. That was just not an option.

My sisters and I now accepted that nothing was an option in this home. We cleaned the house up and down until it was spotless every day. We suffered through the beatings and the games until she decided when it was enough. I learned to close my eyes often, even during the kicking and punching, the hair-pulling and screaming, and pretend I was a beautiful little girl twirling around in a beautiful sundress in a field of flowers, holding the hands of two loving parents who loved me back with my two sisters at my sides. That was the only way to get through the worst of times.

Family Visits
and a Marriage

7

It was a little before our second Christmas in the
home. My sisters and I were about to have a school vacation. Usually
Diane would stay home with us but she now had a job working in a
store close by. My father's mother had promised that one day she
would come and visit us while we were living with our dad. It worked
out that we were out of school for a week and she was going to come
see us during this time. I still can't believe they agreed to the visit.
What a risk—having someone from the *outside* come to the *inside*. I
do remember my father and Diane fighting about her visit before she
arrived. Diane never wanted her to come, for obvious reasons, and
my dad was just trying to make his mom happy by letting her see her
grandchildren. She drove all the way from Wisconsin to stay with us.

My sisters and I were so excited that we would see her. She was
the most cheerful lady you would ever meet. She smelled like flowers
and candy. She would make us laugh and smile and give us anything
we wanted, just like a normal grandma would. But my sisters and I
were a little apprehensive at first, not sure how to act, especially
because we knew Diane hated her. We weren't sure whether to act as
excited as we really were or just stay on our normal courses and stay
low. So, when she arrived we all screamed and jumped for joy silently
in our rooms.

She walked into the house but we weren't allowed to see her until Diane gave us permission. Finally, after she was there for an hour or so, we could hear her begging my dad and stepmom to see us. They allowed us to come out of our rooms.

When I saw her I couldn't contain my true emotions. I was filled with apprehension, relief, excitement, and fear.

Diane snatched my arm and yanked me back into my room. She pointed her finger at me and screeched, "We are NOT happy she is here! She is only here to watch you while we are at work and that's it! Don't try to pull any stunts, understand little girl?" I nodded my head. She grabbed my chin with her strong, dry hand and squeezed tight. "Do you understand!" she howled one more time. The sting crept throughout my entire face. I tried so hard to hold the tears back. I thought maybe we had a chance for freedom.

Diane and I walked out of my room and back into the kitchen where everyone was gathered. I gave grandma a hug and pretended I wasn't ecstatic to see her. I felt relieved she was there. Maybe, just maybe, when dad and Diane were at work I could actually be a happy child. My sisters and I felt a slight glimpse of hope because we thought maybe grandma would see what dad and Diane did to us and would tell someone and we could finally leave this place.

Diane couldn't make it more obvious she hated my grandma. During her entire stay, Diane would walk out of a room as soon as my grandmother entered. Diane gave her dirty looks and interrupted her when she was talking. She would go against anything my grandma did for the three of us.

When my grandma arrived, Ben and Diane told her that we were on a strict diet and she was not allowed to feed us anything. Diane also told her that we were very bad children and weren't allowed to play with any toys. However, during her stay, Diane eased up on us a little bit. We only spent a couple of hours a day in our rooms. We still cleaned the house until it was spotless and received physical abuse, but it was mostly muted and in secret. We didn't eat cereal or any other breakfast, only PB & J for the whole day. It was cheap and gave us something to eat to tide us over until the next day. We never had any milk or fruits or vegetables. My grandma was enraged she couldn't take us to get snacks or make us pancakes in the morning and fought with my father about it until the wee hours of the night.

I could tell my grandma knew there was something wrong. She knew we needed help. But Diane was impossible. My grandmother would argue with Diane about feeding us certain treats or letting us play. My grandma even let us watch television. Diane was enraged. When my father came home Diane made sure she screamed at him loud enough for my grandma to hear. She went on about my grandmother's bad influence on us and how she needed to cut her visit short.

Once day my grandma took us to the library. I was so excited to see the rows and rows of books. I wanted to read all of them. Diane had said we could go but we weren't allowed to check out any books. Grandma said she didn't care, that we were allowed to get as many books as we wanted. That night when Diane came home and saw all of our books she took them away and screamed at my grandma for an hour. Diane told grandma that we didn't deserve to read books.

While I was at the library I wrote my grandma a letter. I wrote her to tell her how glad I was that she was there and to thank her for all the fun we had with her. Grandma took the letter home and put it on the coffee table. When Diane returned home she saw the letter, snatched it off the table and threw it away in the garbage. Diane came in my room and grabbed a hold of my shirt and pinned me up against the bunk bed. I remember her scowling and saying, "How dare you lie to your grandma like that, you little shit! You just wait until she leaves, you're really going to get it then!"

It was only when all of our chores were done that we were allowed to spend time with our grandma. I remember one day after Diane left for work my sisters and I were all hard at work and my grandma demanded we stop so we could go get a Happy Meal from McDonald's. We drove to McDonald's like joyful little happy girls. I had never been happier. I scarfed down a hamburger and French fries and slurped up a Sprite.

Although grandma had instructed us to keep McDonald's a secret, Diane somehow found out. When we came home Diane was waiting for us with rage in her eyes. She came up to me and grabbed the side of my head. She dragged me into the bathroom by my ear. She picked me up and slammed me down on the sink top. She grabbed the back of my head by my hair and titled my head back. She picked up the soap dispenser and put the spout by my lips. I turned my head fast only to meet her other hand grabbing my chin tightly. I knew what was coming and already felt like I was going to vomit. She shoved the end of the dispenser in my mouth and started pumping. And kept pumping. Tears were pouring down my cheeks as my open mouth started to gurgle. Bubbles spewed from my burning mouth. This soap made my stomach churn and I couldn't hold down the McDonald's anymore.

I leaned forward with just enough time for Diane to jump out of the way, and she snarled, "That will teach you to disobey me! Just wait, Grandma is leaving in two days and she won't be here to rescue you anymore, will she!" Diane pushed my head up against the mirror as vomit, tears, and soap sprayed through the tiny bathroom. As she grabbed for the door handle she looked me in the eye with no emotion and screeched with her raspy, heartless voice: "Now you have one minute to clean up this fucking mess!"

One day grandma took my sisters and me to downtown Brighton for a walk. I loved that she made sure we were good and bundled up. She gave us hats, scarves, and mittens to wear. We traveled from store to store, even walked on the bridge at Mill Pond. There were clouds and it was cold out but we didn't care. We were so delighted to be out of the house, walking around with so much to see.

Since Diane had been home that morning, we didn't eat breakfast. My stomach was rumbling the whole time. I just couldn't ignore it. I was afraid to tell grandma because I didn't know what she would do. I knew she wouldn't go off on me or hit me, but I didn't want her to start crying.

We went into a store that had all sorts of toys and candy. It was almost like heaven. There were shelves about the height of me just stacked with candy and treats. It was incredible. I lined myself up with the shelves and realized I could take some of this candy without anyone noticing. I looked to see if anybody was looking. When I realized the coast was clear I took two boxes of Milk Duds from the shelf and shoved them into my mitten. I don't know why I didn't ask grandma to buy them for me, because I know she would have. I just thought I wouldn't take any chances. I saw food and an opportunity to eat, so I took them.

We walked back to Mill Pond to see the ducks. Grandma and I sat down on the bench while my sisters went close to the ice water to see them up close. I felt so guilty about what I had done. I couldn't keep it inside me. It was just something about the gentleness and giving nature of my grandma that I had to tell her what I had done. I took my mitten off with my prized treasures and held them in my open hand. Grandma looked down at me and was confused.

"Jasmine honey, where did you get this candy?"

I didn't know how to tell her I took them; I just couldn't break her heart. I wanted to explain that I was so hungry, and I wanted to eat them, or anything for that matter. I started to cry and just shook my head in disgrace.

I began to cry more and tried to explain but somehow she understood my words. She looked at me and lifted my chin up. She said, "Jasmine, you shouldn't have done that. You should have asked me. I would have bought them for you."

I continued to cry. I felt like my world was crashing down. I wanted her to think I was a good little girl but I just have to eat something. All along we were good little girls and were punished for nothing, and I sit here on this bench knowing I had done something very wrong. I felt terrible. Grandma suggested we return the candy and I sorrowfully agreed. My stomach continued to rumble, louder than before, but I just did what I had learned to do—change the hunger into numbness.

I then realized grandma might tell Diane. I became utterly terrified for a moment. I looked up at her in a panic. She was mumbling to herself about what just happened when she looked down at me and realized why I looked so afraid. She knew the reason. She just wasn't going to say it. I looked up at her in concern and asked, "Grandma, are you going to tell Diane? I'm so sorry."

She looked down at me and said, "Oh no honey, we would never tell Diane something like this. This is something she doesn't need to know. Don't you worry, little one, this stays between you and I."

I felt so relieved. I couldn't believe I actually had an ally. I continued to cry in disbelief. Through teary eyes I watched as my sisters laughed and giggled around the ducks in the pond. I had a sense of hope that we would someday get out of this. We just had to suck it up and ride out the storm.

One day near the end of grandma's visit, I caught her crying in the kitchen. When she saw me she just grabbed me tight and squeezed me with a big, warm hug. I felt so safe. She whispered, "I just love you girls so much, you know that?" At that very moment I knew grandma wasn't going to take us away. I knew Diane was just too much for her. Diane had too much power.

During the last few days of her visit, when dad and Diane were at work, grandma would take us all around the town we lived in. She bought us little treats and snacks and anything else we wanted. We would go to the park or play in playgrounds. It was really cold outside but she said we needed to get out and have some fun. She tried to ignore what dad and Diane did to us when we were at home. She believed there was nothing she could do about it.

On the day that grandma was to leave, I was sitting on The Green Chair when I heard her and Fawna talking. I perked my ears up to listen to them whispering. Fawna was crying and grandma was hugging her. I couldn't really make out what grandma was saying but all of a sudden they let go of each other and there was complete silence throughout the house. Then Fawna cried as she said, "Grandma, we just can't keep living like this." Grandma replied, "I know, honey." It must have been like a thousand knives through her heart at that moment.

While sitting on The Chair I rested my head back against the wall. Tears rolled down my cheeks. I felt like I was a piece of tin foil and someone was crunching me up into a little ball. How much longer do we have to live this awful life? How much longer before someone is smart enough to realize the pain and suffering we endure day in and day out, and how long until they help us escape?

Grandma's visit was almost to an end. My sisters and I tried to secretly plead for her not to leave. She wanted to take us back to Wisconsin, but so many terrible things would have come out of that. She was already in trouble with my father for fighting with Diane so it probably wouldn't have been a good idea. The day she left was a big blur to me, probably because I couldn't bear to think what our lives would be like after she was gone. I knew Diane would make up for lost time. And my guess proved to be correct in no time at all. She made sure we were aware of our roles in this household and the reality of the life she thought we deserved. It wasn't one day before we were painfully reminded of our places. We were going to die in this house.

When my grandma left it was on a particularly cold winter morning and I had never felt emptier. I knew from the beginning of her visit that she probably wasn't going to rescue us, but I at least thought her visit would help us out in *some* way.

Now it was back to the grind, a life we are beginning to live so well. I care about my sisters and nothing else. I eat when I can, stop the pain when I can, and hide when I can. I stay away from Diane at all costs—unless it means she might hunt down one of my sisters. I go to school only to find food and escape the abuse for a few short hours. Yes, I hear the snickers and giggles from the kids in my class but the pain I feel from their bullying amounts to nothing compared to the pain I will feel when I go home. I am an 80-year-old prisoner of war trapped in an 8-year-old body. And there is no hope of getting out of this territory behind enemy lines anytime soon.

My father wouldn't allow anyone on my mother's side of the family to come visit us. That was one thing he didn't have to have Diane convince him on. We weren't even allowed to talk to them on the phone. If my mom, aunts, uncles, or cousins called my dad or Diane would hang up and pull the phone out of the wall. We weren't allowed any contact with anyone related to us. Some relatives tried so hard to see us or even just hear our voices. But that was a privilege we did not have.

One exception was our Uncle Richard. In the beginning my father was adamant that we still keep in touch with him. I like to believe it was because my dad always knew my uncle would be our true savior. Sometimes when he called, Diane would tell him we were in the house about to eat dinner and she would let us catch up with him for a few minutes. We loved talking to him. I always remembered that he had good hearing, so if I talked quietly he would always be able to understand what I would say. I could tell him anything I wanted. I never did though, because I felt forced to pretend like we were happy kids living in a great home with two loving parents. It helped to think, but sometimes made it worse, that Uncle Richard and other foster parents would have had us taken out of that home if they had known what was happening to my sisters and me.

I remember talking to him one time and counting my mosquito bites. I quickly realized the slower I counted, the longer I was allowed to stay on the phone. I think I spent five minutes counting up to 20. I even added a few fake bites to make the time last even longer. He always listened and made me laugh. I could have been talking about anything and he would have been on the other end just listening away with full attention about what I had to say.

Diane hated it when Uncle Richard called because my dad let us talk to him. On the days my uncle called, Diane made sure we paid our dues later for talking to him on the phone. She would have us eat something ridiculous or she would go on an abusive raid, punching and smacking us. After a while our phone conversations to Uncle Richard slowly diminished.

After a year or so social services got intervened in regards to these family visits and informed Diane and my father that our immediate family had the right to see us. They threatened them with court orders but my father and Diane didn't care. Several visits were scheduled with my mother, aunt, and two cousins and my sisters but I never even left the house. Our family members were so excited about seeing the "three little girls of the family," only to be stood up by a coward controlled by a monster. We were never even told about the visits.

After social workers were informed that the visits weren't happening, they stepped in with the court order to allow my mother see us. They coordinated a visit by scheduling a meeting at Mill Pond. The two cousins that were coming along with my mother were like sisters to us. We were very close with them before we moved in with my dad. Their mother was my mom's sister and we spent a lot of time together that I cherished and felt like such a good little girl that was deeply loved.

On a warm spring day we all piled in the car and drove to the park. As we drove nearer I saw my mother first. Even from a distance I could see the anguish and frustration on her face. My father pulled our car up to where they were standing. My sisters and I were crunched together in the back of the Toyota. We weren't allowed to get out.

As we pulled up next to the other family members my father rolled down his window. My aunt started screaming about how they have to let us get out, that it was part of the court order. She and my father started yelling at each other. My cousins just hugged each other and started crying in despair. One of my cousins kept mouthing the words "I love you" to us. During all of the fighting Diane leaned over to the driver's window and yelled, "The girls decided they don't want to see you today!" Fawna just sobbed in the backseat. Diane turned around to the back and screamed for us to look the other way. Everyone was either screaming or crying. My mom was screaming the most and my aunt was trying to calm her down. She didn't look good at all. She was smoking a cigarette and tears were pouring down her cheeks. Her clothes were dirty and hanging off her. I couldn't help but think, even in my 9-year old mind, "Come on Mom, get it together. Pull yourself together so we can come live with you again."

My mom came up close to our car and started pounding on the back window. "Look at me, girls! I know you want to see me and they won't let you! I love you! I...love....you!"

I looked over at Cam as she wept. I was sitting in the middle and my two sisters were sobbing on each side of me. I finally wiped away a stream of tears trickling down my face and looked out the window away from my mom. I just looked up at the sky.

My dad has had enough. He rolls up his window and speeds off. The last sight burned into my mind is my cousin crying and reaching her hand out to stop the car. I wanted to get out so badly and run up to them and never look back. I knew they would have saved me right then and there.

Diane sat in the front seat cackling. She finally collected herself and turned around and snarled, "So you see now that nobody wants you? Nobody would ever want such ugly pieces of shit."

All I could think about was how much that hurt them to not even get to hug us—how they drove all the way to see us and couldn't even give us a hug. I went home that night and erased many people out of my memory. I knew that from now on I needed to stop thinking of people I once knew of, because nobody loved us enough to save us. I finally gave in and believed Diane. I erased my mother, my aunts, my cousins, even my Uncle Richard from my memory. I no longer knew of these people, because they no longer knew of me.

Twice during the two years with my father, my dad's half-brother visited us. He didn't stay long but always came with our Aunt Michelle. Diane hated them too, but she was much more cordial to them. She was rude and didn't acknowledge their presence but at least treated them with some decency. My father seemed happy when his brother and his wife were in town. He would let them take us for car rides and let us have hours away from home.

On one visit they brought a movie called *The Dark Crystal.* It was made in 1982 but my uncle swore it was one of the best movies of all time. It is a science-fiction movie set about a thousand years ago with puppet characters who have to piece together this crystal to save the planet. It gave me the creeps to watch it but somehow I grew to love this movie. Uncle Jeff would sit down with Cam and me and explain the movie parts that we didn't understand. It was one of the very few movies that we ever watched while we lived there.

After we watched the movie one night I dreamed of being in some science-fiction film. I realized that all these little dreams that I had made my days go by faster. Whether it was twirling around in a field of flowers or thinking I needed to put together a crystal puzzle to escape the wrath of an evil stepmother, these dreams kept me going. They gave me an energy I desperately needed to make it to the next day.

I can vividly remember one of the last times we saw my aunt and uncle. They took my sisters and me to McDonald's on their last night. They bought us each a little ice cream sundae cup with caramel on top. It was the only food we ate that day. We pulled into a parking spot and stayed there to devour our special treat. We talked about how awful Diane was. I hoped they didn't know what she did to us. They knew she was a dreadful woman, but I knew they were leaving the next day and weren't taking us with them. I just couldn't stop crying. I don't even remember if my aunt and uncle knew that I cried in the seat behind them. I didn't even want to finish my ice cream even though I hadn't eaten all day. I guess it was because when I had lost all hope, I began to lose my appetite too.

In the winter of my second-grade year, my father and Diane decided to officially get married. We weren't told anything that was going on. All I can remember about the decision was something right before the marriage. I was sitting in my room and they were both looking at a big calendar on the wall. They were both very interested in it, and I could tell they were trying to make something work. Later we found out they were planning a four-day trip to Florida to get married and have a short honeymoon.

On the night we left for Florida, Diane packed all of our bags. She told us we were taking a road trip. I found it odd we were leaving in the middle of the night. We piled into the car and headed off. I was quite awake. I asked my dad where we were going and he replied, "a road trip." I was smart enough to know how to read road signs and try to figure out where we were going.

When we started off I thought maybe we were going to stay with Uncle Richard. He lived near Canton, Michigan. But we were on a different journey, through Canton, Ohio. We kept on driving. I finally grew tired and my eyes were too exhausted to read any more signs. I fell asleep on Cam's shoulder to the song *Shadows of the Night* by Pat Benatar. I liked to sing along in my head and pretend I was a shadow in the night and all my dreams would come true in the end.

I was angry the entire drive to Florida. In school we were doing a play called *James and the Giant Peach*. I was the ladybug and got to wear a cute little costume and get my face painted for it. To learn my part I wrote out all my lines 100 times. I actually had made a few friends while rehearsing for the play and felt excited to have friends for the first time. I memorized my lines perfectly, and was never more excited in my life with the chance to show off my great acting skills to all of the parents. I was furious in the car after I realized that because of this trip I wasn't going to be in the school play. I was good for nothing.

The next morning I awoke to a quiet car. *Crash into Me* by the Dave Matthews Band softly played on the radio. For some reason, that to this day I still don't understand, his voice made me feel scared.

Twenty-five hours after we started, we arrived in Ormond Beach, Florida. All I had eaten the entire time was a hash brown from McDonald's. I didn't care, though, because it was the best food I had eaten in a long time.

Ormond Beach was where Diane's mom lived. The plans turned out to be that my sisters and I were supposed to stay with her. Diane's mother was actually a nice lady who would give you anything. During our stay she always made us smile and played games with us and was quite pleasant.

When we arrived at her house, Diane's mom came running out to help us out of the car and squeeze us half to death. She really did love us. It's hard to believe such a satanic woman spawned from such an angel. The first day we were there she took us for a drive to see more of Florida. It was exciting. I couldn't believe how warm it was. We got to put on shorts and tank tops that this grandma bought us.

She drove us in a convertible on the beach. We parked on the sand right next to the hotel that dad and Diane were staying at. We joked about how the waves come in and could scoop you out into the ocean. Grandma told us a story about how that actually did happen to her friend's van. The day was cloudy and misting a little bit. Grandma kept apologizing and saying she wished it was warmer so we could go swimming but I didn't care. This was the best vacation ever.

On the night that dad and Diane got married we all went to a fancy restaurant with an outside deck that was on the water. There were all these pretty lights strung from the ceiling and poles on the edge of the dock. I wished we didn't have to go home. I could have stayed there all winter long. Grandma bought us these cute outfits to wear to the wedding and I felt like a princess in mine. It was a black top and a matching black skort that had pretty white flowers all over and lace on the hem. I heard the minister marrying them during the ceremony but we weren't allowed to watch. Dad and Diane were really happy and smiling a lot.

It was a really good night for my sisters and me. We were acting like a real family. It's too bad it was all a lie. Diane knew that after they said "I do" she would have complete and total control over us, even more so than before. Any chance we had to escape was fading away like the waves under the dock going back out into the cold, dark ocean.

We returned home in Michigan four days later. Diane now knew she was ruler of all. Even my father. Things were about to get worse. Dad worked even more hours for taking so many days off and I hardly ever saw him anymore. Our now official stepmother controlled our every move and action. Life was over for us.

Deeper in Hell 8

We sucked it up. We never once stood up for ourselves or disobeyed what we were told. We just tuned out every scream and yell so our eardrums wouldn't bust. We just tensed up for every blow or smack so that we couldn't feel the complete sting. Every absurd and ridiculous stunt that Diane pulled we just blocked out so that we didn't lose our minds and go completely insane. But we were right on the edge of insanity.

My sisters and I found ways to jump Diane's obstacles and defeat her. One thing we did was sign words to each other. We would sit on The Green Chair or in our rooms and lean over so that we could see each other. We didn't know sign language so we developed our own. We made letters out of our hands to eventually create a word. I remember laughing on the inside about how funny it was when Fawna signed to me, "Diane is ugly." I think she almost heard me. I didn't care, though. Plus, it was the truth.

We actually got really good at our letter language. We could sign words pretty quickly to each other and just laugh and giggle, in complete silence of course. Sometimes we signed to warn each other, like when Diane was in the kitchen creating a toxic mixture to use for her afternoon exploitation. I remember doing it right behind her back, as if she wasn't even there. She was so stupid. She didn't think we were smart enough to talk about her when she was three feet in front of us.

Then there was the issue with food. Usually it was still peanut butter and jelly sandwiches, puffed wheat, or nothing. On occasion Ben and Diane would make split pea soup. Those words just make me cringe. Dad would spend all day making it. It tasted awful. I would rather drink the liquid soap.

All the soup ingredients together were a horrible mix. Dad made gallons of it at a time. Whatever we didn't eat for dinner that night he sealed into gallon plastic bags and placed them in the freezer. The house reeked of this horrid concoction. It consisted of split peas, carrots, ham, and onions. Dad would stand there for hours huddling over the pots, making sure it was "perfect." But it was dreadful. I would cry at the stench of this soup and my whole body would cringe. The taste itself was not the worst part, and after all, it was food. But it was just how much we had to eat. We had to eat it for weeks at a time. It made my stomach churn just to look at it. Diane would stand there and make sure we swallowed every spoonful. I felt like taking my bowl and launching it at her face.

On rare occasions for dinner when pea soup was unavailable we were given chicken pot pie. The first night we were served this I was so excited. I thought maybe times were changing, as if they wanted to start loving us and treating us like normal children. Again, I was proven wrong.

The chicken pot pie was appalling. The edges were always burnt and crumbly. The inside looked like watery butter. We never got to eat the pot pie hot. No matter how hungry we were, we tried to avoid this horrible excuse of a meal. Sometimes during dinner, if Diane was watching her television shows, we tried to disguise our meal as if it were gone. All three of us sat at the table with our little chicken pot pie in purple plastic cups pretending to gobble it up. At first, Diane had no idea we were really not eating it. Fawna figured out to chew it big bites at a time and pretend to wash it down with some water. Cam and I were always so jealous because we had to eat more than her. Fawna's tactic was usually pretty effective, with the exception of one instance that is burned into my memory.

Diane walked quietly back into the kitchen behind Fawna's back. She held her pointer finger over her mouth, signaling us not to peep a word. Fawna realized she was there and lowered her cup slowly. Diane hovered over her in intimidation and authority. Fawna lifted her head up and that's when it happened.

Diane took a large stomp closer to Fawna's backside. She lifted her hand and, before I knew it, Fawna's face was slammed against the kitchen table. She then slammed it again and again. She just stood there, banging Fawna's face into the side of the table. Fawna was screaming and trying to reach behind her to make Diane stop. Cam turned away and screamed. I covered my face and sobbed. I thought Fawna was going to die. Soon blood splattered on the table and floor. I wanted to scream. I could feel anger in my hands and was seconds away from jumping out of my chair to choke that woman to death.

She wasn't done yet. She slammed Fawna's face one last time and then pulled her head up by her hair. I looked up to see Fawna's face, black and blue and covered in blood. Diane screamed in her ear about how stupid Fawna was. She screamed, "You think you're smarter than me, do you!?"

Fawna was limp and her eyes rolled back in her head. Diane then picked up the purple cup in disgust and screamed some more. Fawna was going in and out of consciousness.

After a minute Diane turned to Fawna and sneered, "What's the matter, Fawna Lynn, you don't like this meal I slaved over? What the hell is the matter with you, ugly shit! Now drink this before I bash your head in again!"

Fawna didn't even have enough strength to cry. I could tell she was trying to. Her head was bobbing around like a doll's. Diane handed Fawna the cup and Fawna dropped it. Some of the chicken pot pie mush splattered onto the floor. Diane demanded Camai cleaned up the mess immediately. I sat in my chair and just wept. Was this real? How could this be happening to us? What did we do to deserve this? I just didn't understand.

Diane now stood over Cam, screaming at her while she cleaned up the kitchen floor. Diane released her grasp on Fawna's head and stood with her arms crossed and all the weight on one hip. She screamed, "I'm going to stand here until we finish our dinner, is that clear?"

Camai was crying and trying to clean up the floor as best she could. I was praying this tirade would be over soon so I could look at Fawna and make sure she was okay. Fawna finally gained enough strength to hold the cup but her head was still wobbling around. I closed my eyes, but when I opened them I was still in this hell. Fawna was drinking her already chewed disgusting burnt soggy chicken pot pie. Tears were rolling down her face but she was lifeless. I couldn't believe what I was seeing. Just when I thought it couldn't get any worse.

My dad never really abused us like Diane did. He would smack us around and spank us with belts and sticks when he got home from work but he didn't get as violent as Diane did. Instead, he did things that got to us emotionally. Not only would Diane have us tell him that we hated him but she would make him hate us as well.

At one point, a social worker ordered that we all visit a family therapist. After a few months my stepmom and father found one that would work for their "hectic" schedules. The only reason the three of us liked to go see the therapist was because he got us out of the house for two hours each week. He also read us stories. I didn't really know what to think because he tape-recorded us. I knew deep down he wasn't going to save us. He wasn't smart enough. Just like the social workers. I mean, why spend time doing paperwork, asking questions, and making sure children are safe if you don't have to?

Every time we went there he started with all of us in the room together. He asked us how we all were and how things were going at home. My father and Diane put on a great show: "Oh, things are going really well, we are finally starting to bond and act as a family." My sisters and I would just nod and look away. After our family visit he would tell dad and Diane to step out of the room while he counseled with us. He never asked us questions about dad and Diane. He never asked if they hurt us or if we were fed three good meals and some snacks each day. Instead, he read stories to us about bunny rabbits and fairy tales.

My sisters and I just sat there, crunched together on this soft couch, with empty lives. We didn't know what to do with ourselves. Our eyes were glazed over and our hearts were scarred. Our stomachs were empty and our energy was drained. We were robots to the rest of the world.

After our story time, the therapist told my sisters and me to go wait in the lobby while he talked with dad and Diane. We just sat there for a while, our heads hanging low and our spirits even lower.

Since the social worker had told the therapist that we were bad kids, he recommended that we start what he called a "point system." Basically, if you did something good such as complete a household chore you received 15 points. If you acted out or disobeyed, you lost points. This translated to, if you gave Diane a dirty look or tensed up when she hit you, you lost 20 points. It was pretty much set up as a lose-lose situation. We would never win.

The therapist said if we reach a certain goal, such as 100 points, that dad and Diane would take us to the park or for some other fun day out. I just let that little idea go right in one ear and out the other. If Diane had complete control of the point system, which she would, 100 points was just a hazy mirage in a hot dessert.

It was around this time in our stay that the broomstick became notorious. Diane would order us to bend over at staggered times of the day and beat us with the stick. That stick hurt just as much as the black belt. It stung with every blow. She liked to hit me on the back of my knees or my upper legs. I was left with welts and bruises. It didn't matter if the marks were visible; we still went to school and our teachers and friends pretended as if they didn't see any of it. Kids moved away when I went to sit with them or play with them on the playground. Nobody wanted to be friends with a smelly girl covered in bruises. I just wanted to be with my sisters. They understood.

The way the point system worked in reality, Cam was always in the hole. If you got in the hole, you got a beating. That means Camai got it all the time, on top of what Diane already routinely did. I was sometimes in the hole. But there was a point in time where I was at plus-81 points. I was so proud of myself. The chart was posted on the side of the refrigerator, so when you sat in The Green Chair you could examine it. I studied the chart up and down for hours. I tried to see where I lost points and where I gained them. I tried to learn from the chart, but everything Diane did was clearly not a pattern, and I never got to 100.

I felt so bad for Cam; I don't think she was ever out of the hole. I wanted to help her. Maybe give her some of my points. We must have had the point system for months. Our therapist would review our point totals when we visited him each week and tell us what to work on. He would always tell us not to yell at Diane or throw temper tantrums. He didn't know what he was talking about. I never listened to him anyway. He didn't listen to us. I didn't care what he had to say. He was just another person whose job it was to protect us and completely failed.

Dad continued to drain us mentally. Every day he told us to stay out of Diane's way and to respect her. He would shuffle off to work and it was hell from there. He told us that he loved her and wanted us to love her, too; that if we kept acting up and being bad that he would lose her. I just wanted to make him happy. I tried to stay on my best behavior. I felt like I didn't even care if the price was my life. I begged for his approval.

Once he received five tickets to attend the circus that was in town. I was so excited. My sisters and I signed our letter language to each other about it all day when Diane wasn't around. Diane caught Fawna and I looking at each other. She didn't do anything, surprisingly. However, when dad came home that evening she told him we were *really* bad that day. She said that we threw fits and yelled at her and even asked for our real mom.

My dad was outraged, absolutely infuriated. He told all of us to line up in the kitchen. My sisters and I stood side by side—like soldiers in boot camp. We hung our heads and clasped our hands behind our backs. I was shaking because I was scared by whatever was about to happen. My dad pulled the tickets out of his back pocket and a lighter from his front pocket. He yelled at us about being bad and lit the circus tickets on fire. He threw them into the sink while they burned. My sisters and I were crying.

We sobbed and begged for our own father's approval, pleading with our eyes for him to forgive us. He hit us each a couple of times, a smack here, a punch here. I didn't even care he was hitting me. I was getting dizzier with every hit but all I focused on was those damn circus tickets. As they burned away to ash in the sink I felt as if I was burning down to the ground.

At this moment I realized I had nothing else to lose. My sisters and I were done. We had to keep holding on to each other in order to stay alive and stay sane. We weren't bad children. We were polite and respectful and rarely disobeyed orders, unless we had to stay alive or unharmed. If we did act out it was because we had to. If we weren't perfect it was because we sometimes couldn't be because we were protecting ourselves.

Why did everyone think we were such awful kids? Why did the social workers not even attempt to remove us from the home? Why did our teachers and principal have us on the bad list at school? Does God hate us? Is there even a God? What did we do to deserve this? Nobody deserves this. And we all knew it wasn't even close to being over. There still was no light at the end of the tunnel.

When it came to school, it wasn't an escape for us anymore. It didn't make a difference if we were there or not. My third-grade teacher was actually compassionate and sympathetic about my bumps and bruises but never did anything about the situation. I think she knew what was going on, in fact, I know she knew. The fact that she didn't say anything is what upsets me.

I didn't really have any friends; I was afraid to. I thought that if they found out about Diane that they would tell their mommies and daddies, and I wouldn't make it out of there alive. I didn't want other kids to know. Besides, they didn't care anyways.

During recess I played by myself and just minded my own business. A lot of kids made fun of me. They teased me about the clothes I wore or how I smelled. They would call me "Skinny Jasminnie" or poke fun at my ugly haircut and the bruises all over my body. At lunchtime, because most of the kids knew about my lunchbox raids, they would hold their lunchboxes next to their chests and guard them with their lives. They stared me down as I walked by with my stomach growling and my heart barely beating.

Our school received a new playground structure during my third-grade year. Since I played by myself I didn't care if anybody was watching when I played on it every day. I tried to be cool by walking on the top of the monkey bars, dancing around like I was on top of the world. Some girls actually thought I was cool because I could do that. I did it every day, sometimes even for a crowd. It was such a good feeling. Most of the kids lost interest but I still did it for the sake of self-dignity.

On one muggy day everything was sticky and all the metal on the playground was slippery. I stood up on the new monkey bars and started my little routine, dancing to the popular song, *Lovefool* by The Cardigans. I took two or three steps before the bars became too slippery to hop all the way across. I couldn't turn back and became stuck. I didn't know what to do, so I started to slowly walk back to the beginning so I safely could get off. My foot slipped right off the next step and in what felt like slow motion I went from a standing position to landing on my crotch on top of the monkey bars.

Everyone was already running inside from recess. I was thankful for this. My eyes welled up with tears instantaneously and I felt like I had landed on a bomb. I couldn't believe how much pain I was in. It was burning so bad. I didn't know what to do. I was crying and wailing from pain while the teachers continued to blow the whistle for everyone to go inside. One of the first-grade teachers walked over and told me I needed to get inside right away before I got in trouble. She noticed I was crying and asked if I needed help. I told her I hurt myself on the bar and I couldn't move. She slowly helped me down and walked me to the nurse's office. Every step I took felt like knives. I was crying and begging that someone would carry me.

I lay down on the cot in the nurse's office and positioned myself to somehow mask the pain. I was rolling around and continued to cry for an hour. They called Diane while she was at work and she came in two hours later. The nurse explained to her what happened and told Diane to check me and make sure everything was okay down there.

As soon as I saw Diane my pain went away. I didn't want her to touch me. All I could think about was what would happen because I had hurt myself. Maybe she would lighten up and not make me do so many chores the next day. I so badly wished a social worker would come soon because I trusted them more to make sure I was okay than Diane.

She took me into the bathroom, where I pulled my pants down. There was blood in my underwear and I was already bruising. She looked at me like I was a piece of garbage. She squatted down and looked at my private parts for a second. I rolled my eyes because I knew this was all an act. It was so uncomfortable. Finally she spoke. She used her scratchy and uncompassionate tone. "You're fine. Don't think for one second you'll get out of your chores at home." I cried some more as I looked up in her eyes. She sneered at me and then lifted her hand to smack me. I flinched only for her to grab my chin and proclaim, "You make sure you come home right after school because it will probably take you longer to finish your chores, little girl." I bent over slowly and pulled my pants up, making sure to be careful of my injury.

She opened the door of the bathroom and gave the nurse a pleasant look and fake smile. She said, "She'll be fine. It doesn't look like she did any damage. Thanks for taking care of her, I really appreciate it."

"That's crap Diane, you don't give a damn," I thought. I bowed my head and slowly crept back to class. It was burning and throbbing and I couldn't even dodge the pain a little bit. I spent almost a week in pain, barely able to sit or stand. Somehow I managed to take all my beatings and torture along with completing all of my chores, heaven forbid I don't clean her house for one day.

My dad really liked to cook. He experimented by making many different types of meals and recipes. Except for that horrible split pea soup, we rarely got to taste anything he made. But I also hated it when he cooked because it put Diane in this mood of completely insanity. She would dance around the house and glare at us as if we were ghosts. She just rubbed it in that she was about to eat the most delicious thing she had ever eaten in her entire life. She knew we wanted to eat what our father had made—or anything for that matter—so badly. That was why it was fun for her to taunt us like Satan does to his souls.

Our lips quivered and mouths drooled as we fought to remain quiet in our seats. I watched my dad as he swayed back and forth to a song he was singing in his head. I wanted to smile but I was afraid I might get in trouble.

One time he cut up a radish to make it look like a rose in just ten seconds. He let me hold it for a few minutes and told me it wasn't nearly as pretty as me. He said, "That is why we named you Jasmine Rose. Because you are so beautiful."

He loved to make desserts; they were his specialty. He would dip strawberries in creamy milk chocolate perfectly to make them appear as a dessert entrée from a five-star restaurant. Diane would hurry over and snatch one and seductively eat it in front of him. They looked at each other like they were naked. It made me sick. He smiled and just kept bopping back and forth to the song still playing in his head. He was so confident in his work. His brilliance and skill made it impossible for me to take my eyes off him. I wanted to be like him. Not happy or healthy—I wanted to be successful and proud. Those thoughts were just wishful thinking. Because I was ugly and stupid, and I knew I would never amount to anything.

One weekend my dad experimented with pancake batter by making miniature pancakes. He added flavors like cinnamon, peanut butter, and bananas. The pancakes were perfectly shaped, the size of half-dollars, and made the house smell like a bakery. I bet he could have made millions marketing them. The morning my dad made these Diane was at the grocery store. It was my day to sit in The Green Chair. It was hot outside and my legs were sticking to the leather. My dad was dancing so much I could almost hear the music. He made several batches of these delicacies before he glanced over at me with a smile. I knew he was going to let me try one. My mouth salivated like a dog begging for food.

He motioned with his head for me to come stand by him. I stood up and walked slowly to the stove with my head lowered toward the floor. It was the same stove that I was burned on one Saturday. He had such a happy look on his face, as if he was completely content with every aspect of his life.

He picked up a pancake and said, "Open your mouth, kiddo." I picked my head up with stars in my eyes. Drool was pouring down the side of my mouth. My stomach was screaming to snatch it out of his hand, this pancake being the first thing I was eating that day. He gently spoke again, "This one is cinnamon." I ate it in a heartbeat and almost collapsed from the amazing taste.

I got to try all the flavors. He told me to return to The Green Chair and be good until Diane got home. I wanted to grab the plate of pancakes and shove them all at my mouth at once. I watched as he carefully packed them into little sandwich bags. He could have been a millionaire.

Dad and Diane's relationship was slowly distancing. When we first moved in they were love-stricken, absolutely head over heels for each other. They giggled and laughed nonstop. Dad constantly picked Diane up and she straddled him while they shared passionate kisses. We weren't allowed to watch them but I could still see them out of the corner of my eye. As time went on, they grew farther apart. Their disagreements concerning discipline and constant pressure from social workers to make us work as a family began to create tension between the two. Diane was now working at her job more and dad worked all day too. Dad must have been getting sick of coming home every night and having Diane screaming at him, telling him how awful his children are. He knew deep down we weren't bad kids. Diane continued to abuse us in front of him. He never said anything and turned his head, but I could tell it bothered him. I'd like to think it actually tore him apart. Not enough to stop it, though.

Sometimes when Diane was going off on one of us he would come in and tell her to leave us alone. Sometimes he would come in and he would physically make her stop beating us. One time while she was hitting Cam and I he came in and had to drag her out of the room. She was kicking and flailing around. I wanted to laugh but I knew that we were in for it as soon as dad left for work the next morning. It was a vicious cycle. After a long day in that house we would try to sleep at night only to hear the two of them screaming at each other. The abuse between the two of them started to get more frequent, too. It was hard to think about how much we went through during the day and then to hear that during the night. At this point in my life I was completely empty and so drained that I didn't even care. I just rolled over and thought about how I could get to my next source of food. "Good, kill each other. Then we can leave this hellhole," I thought to myself. It didn't really stop. Every night it was the same thing. Just a bunch of yelling and hitting. It was unbearable.

One day in November my sisters and I were ordered to rake the backyard. We went outside and immediately started raking the backyard. We each had a rake and a tarp to drag the leaves around. We spent hours raking the yard. We weren't smart enough to form a strategy to efficiently rake the leaves into a pile. We all split up the yard and made our own piles. I remember Fawna was yelling at me because I seemed to be making more of a mess than when we had started.

After a few hours I looked at my hands. They were blistered and raw. One of my blisters was bleeding and stung really bad. I was sweating now and it was making me even colder. I stood up to take a break. My lower back was aching and I couldn't feel my toes. I wanted to go inside so bad. But we had a job to finish.

For one second I thought we could actually have some fun in the leaves. Maybe dad and Diane would let us play in the piles? Yeah, right, what was I thinking? We used the big blue tarps to form one huge pile in the backyard. We filled up five big brown bags. I could barely even see the tops. We had to put them on their sides and sweep the leaves in. It was hard work for an eight-year-old. Even for ten-year-old Fawna.

Fawna always did protect us. I looked up to her more than anyone. She was the closest thing to a mom we ever had. She really did take the brunt of all of it. She was the first person that Diane went to.

Fawna never really screamed or yelled when she was being hit, just tensed up her face and cried. If Camai and I ever did anything wrong, Fawna would take the blame right away. She was the mother we never had, and most of the time our saving grace. My sisters and I still stuck together. We knew we had to get out. We just had to figure out how.

Operation Runaway 9

Like I said, I always looked up to Fawna. So did Camai. Anything she told us to do, we did. She always got us out of bad situations. She took the blame for things she didn't do. I was so proud to see her in school. I wanted to show off to all the kids who made fun of me that I had a cool big sister. Sometimes I screamed her name when I saw her and waved fiercely. She always smiled but never waved back. Who wants to claim a dorky, beat-up, smelly younger sister anyway?

At this point in our lives, we had a babysitter come watch us in the mornings before school. Diane told our babysitter that we had already eaten breakfast before he had gotten there and that we weren't allowed to play with any toys or have any fun. It was this 60-year-old man who watched us for the two hours before we went to school. He had brown hair with spare grey throughout, and big round glasses. He didn't really talk much and we didn't talk to him. He just told us to get our bags ready for school and that we needed to start walking on time or else we would be late. We never had a real conversation but I always thought he was nice. At least he didn't hit us. My sisters and I loved it when he came before school. He would sit in the family room right outside our rooms and watch the Catholic channel for an hour and a half. We did whatever we wanted. We were always quiet but played games like freeze tag and monkeys on the bed in our rooms. It was our "happy time." He would knock politely after his program was finished and nicely tell us to get ready for school.

My sisters and I always talked about running away. The dreams we imagined in our heads soon became reality when we shared them with each other. We said we didn't care about where we would live, that anything would be better than here. We joked about it every day when we walked to school, about where we could go, who would take us, what would happen next. I imagined living in the local grocery store, or in a garage next to a vacant home. Thinking of living in a garage was exhilarating. I wanted to live in a garage so bad. I would be a good roommate for my sisters. We could play games and take turns making dinner. I would go into the grocery store and we could live off road salt for days at a time. My sisters and I got so excited talking about leaving the hellhole we lived in. We smiled so big at the possibility that Diane would not be a part of our lives anymore.

One day on the way to school, Fawna told us to really think about living somewhere else. We started as usual making jokes about it, about living in garages and boxes on the street. She explained to us that she was serious and she might know somewhere we could run away to. She said we needed to keep quiet and pay attention to any details she might have. It was time to seriously consider the possbiblity of leaving Ben and Diane.

My mind flooded with thoughts and visions of actually living somewhere without Diane, with food and water, no chores, no beatings, whippings, smacks, slaps, kicks, hits, blood, and tears. How lucky would we be? Our time had finally come. We could actually leave and dad and Diane could get on with their lives without us. The world would be a great place. I thought about getting my teacher involved. I knew she would help us get food and water. This could actually work.

I patiently waited for Fawna to give me any details, but a few weeks went by without a word about it. On the way to school one day I mentioned maybe telling my teacher about it because I know she would help us.

Fawna stopped in her tracks and grabbed my arm tight. "Jas! You listen to me right now. You don't breathe a word of this to anyone, you hear me? It is going to work, I'm just waiting for the right time!" I was confused and excited at the same time. I definitely didn't want to make her mad but I wanted more details. This was my life too! And my sisters weren't leaving without me. Just like I would never leave without them.

Fawna had a pretty close friend in her fifth-grade class that she was pretty close with. She had confided in her with very vague details and requested some form of help. As we learned later, this girl had told Fawna that we could live in a shed in her backyard until we found somewhere else to live. The shed was in the very back of the yard. We would get up very early in the morning and stay out very late at night to make sure her parents never knew we were living there. We had a plan for food, water, even personal hygiene. We were actually going to live in a shed.

I didn't even hesitate on agreeing whether or not it was a good idea. Camai and I were ecstatic and we giggled as we planned our great getaway. We talked about everything we would bring. Fawna told us to keep very quiet about it at home. She said we shouldn't even whisper about it. We talked about it only on the way to or from school. I never met the girl whose shed we were going to live in, but Fawna said she was nice and was planning on bringing us food and some other things out to the shed every night. All we needed was a can opener for our meals.

The plan took weeks to map out perfectly. Our arrangement was foolproof. Nobody was going to find out. Dad and Diane would come home to an empty house and wouldn't be able to do one thing about it. It was perfect.

The plan consisted of three steps:

1) **The morning stage.** When dad and Diane left for work, we would already be awake, waiting for them to leave. As soon as we were sure that they had both left we would begin packing right away. We would take all the canned food from our kitchen and distribute it into three duffel bags and backpacks. That way we were each carrying an equal load. We would pack as much warm clothes as possible to last us throughout the winter. When our babysitter was watching his program Fawna would go into the kitchen and take the can opener. We would also pack our toothbrushes, toothpaste, and lots of toilet paper. We would have everything ready to go well before we had to leave for school. While our babysitter watched his television program we would sneak behind the couch with our duffel bags and place them on the side of the house that he couldn't see. We would stuff our backpacks with as much necessary items for survival as possible. When it was time to head down the front porch we would nonchalantly grab our duffel bags and head to school. Fawna instructed us to carry them like they were just full of sports equipment. We were not to draw any attention to ourselves, or the plan could be completely compromised.

2) **The school stage.** During the school day we were to "lay low" and not speak one word to anyone. We would continue our day like any other typical day. We would store our duffel bags with the backpacks, and if anyone asked about them we would say we were leaving for vacation after school. When the school day was

over we would grab our duffel bags and head to the bus loop. Fawna's friend would meet up with us by the bus and tell us what to do next. I remember wanting to know further details but Fawna said it would be best if we knew as little as possible. That way, if anything were to go wrong we really didn't know anything.

3) **The bus and final stage.** We were to get on our friend's bus with our bags and find the closest seat to sit down immediately. Fawna told us to put our heads down so the bus driver wouldn't see us and get suspicious. We were going to ride the bus to Fawna's friend's stop and get off and immediately, and nonchalantly, and head for the shed in her backyard before her parents got home. We would wait to make sure nobody saw us. Freedom.

Our plan was perfect. All we had to do now was wait for the perfect day.

It was a cold winter morning. We knew it was the day. Operation Runaway was in full effect. I woke up and could tell that fresh snow had just fallen. We were all lying awake in our beds. It was around four or five when our dad left for work. I was so excited and nervous at the same time that I didn't know what to do with myself. I was scared that we would get caught by the babysitter. Or that we would never even get on the bus. I was excited that this would be my last morning in this prison.

I just laid there wide awake with thoughts racing through my mind. I could tell Camai was awake, too, as I kept hearing her cough. I didn't say anything to her, trying to follow Fawna's strict orders. I knew Diane hadn't left for work yet so I tried to stay completely still. I wasn't sure if she was in the mood for one of her morning beatings. You never knew with that woman. She was crazy. My heart was beating so fast. I continued to review the plan over and over in my head so that when it became game time I wouldn't mess up and ruin the whole thing.

Diane must have been running late this morning because she didn't even open the door to see if she could smack around one of us before she left. I was really tired from a sleepless night being so anxious. The sun was creeping through my window more and more as it rose, and it helped keep me awake. I heard Diane talking to our babysitter for a minute and the door slam behind her. I looked out my window and saw her backside walking away. I had this great feeling, seeing her walk away. I felt as if I were on top of the world. The sun never felt so warm. I hoped it would be the last time I saw her. I prayed I never saw her face again.

I took a deep breath and reviewed the plan one last time. "This is it, no turning back now," I thought. I rolled over and slowly dropped down from the top bunk. I shook Camai but she was already awake. "It's time. Let's start to pack." She nodded and gave me a small smile. I felt warmth in my heart. Fawna soon snuck in our room and quietly closed the door behind her. She put her back up against it and let out a deep sigh. She then sat on the floor and began folding some clothes. The warmth in my heart now moved to happiness in my soul. Today is the day we will never be hurt again. We will eat, we will smile, we will love. Our childhood as we knew it was about to completely change.

It was getting brighter every minute so we had to move fast. We didn't want the babysitter walking in by chance and seeing us packing everything we owned. I packed most of my clothes; there weren't many. I packed three pairs of pants, two sweaters, a few t-shirts, socks, underwear, and a training bra. I was shaking because I was so scared. The anticipation consumed me as I tried to compose myself.

We finished with our clothes. Fawna crept over to the door and cracked it open. She signaled for us to come over. She opened the door slowly. We all walked out and said good morning to our babysitter. We waved, avoided eye contact, and all casually split into different directions. Fawna went into the kitchen and took the can opener. Camai and I went into the bathroom and took our toothpaste, toothbrushes, and six rolls of toilet paper. We snuck back into our room where Fawna was already packing the kitchen utensils. We finished packing our duffel bags and zipped them up. Now it was time to wait. I wanted to go back to sleep so badly but Fawna wouldn't let me.

After a half hour or so we turned the light off and snuck behind the couch where our babysitter was sitting. I have no idea how we opened the front door and put the bags out without him hearing. He must have been in a deep prayer or something. Our three bags were just sitting there, next to the side of the house, on top of the frost and snow.

On this particular morning there was ice covering the trees. I remember stopping before returning back inside the house to gaze at how pretty all the ice was. I could see my breath.

My sisters and I met in our room for one last time. We talked quietly about the day. My heart jumped when the man knocked on the door for us to leave for school. We shared one big hug and then headed out the door with our backpacks full of things. I couldn't believe it was actually happening. As soon as we got outside we snatched our duffel bags and began the hike to school.

When we got to school I shoved my bag next to the cubbies. My teacher asked why I had two bags that day. I told her it was because I had gymnastics practice right after school. I always wanted to be a gymnast, to be able to do all those flips and spins around a gym. I would feel so cool and like a girl my age should feel. Instead my extracurricular activities consisted of dishes or scrubbing a bathroom until it sparkled.

I took a quick walk to Fawna's classroom during the day. I felt uneasy and was very nervous that our plan was going to fall through. I kept replaying the conversation with my teacher over in my head. If I screw this up I'll never be able to forgive myself. I can't let my sisters down. We need to escape to live.

I stood outside Fawna's classroom and peered in the window, and finally spotted her quietly listening to the teacher. As soon as I saw her I felt giddy yet uneasy. She glanced over to see me waving at her but her face tensed up and she signaled me to go away. Her eyes were big and she seemed upset I was there. I walked back to my class even more nervous than before. What if had I ruined it?

I was so scared during school that day. My fear was fueled by the image of the monster back home. The image of her satanic grin and violent hand coming at me was branded in my mind. There is no way we can turn back now. Even if we changed our mind, Diane would see us return with all of our belongings and know what we were up to. We would surely die.

The end of the school day finally came. We were ready to initiate the most important step yet. We met up with Fawna's friend outside the school. It was cloudy and small snowflakes fell around us. The girl was really pretty. She had long brown hair and a sweet face. She smelled like cinnamon and floral shampoo. I wanted to hug her. I was almost in tears of happiness that we would never return to that home again. They wouldn't know where to find us. I wished I could see their faces as they came home to an empty house and three girls who would never return again. It didn't seem real. Camai and I were holding hands and almost jumping up and down. She was smiling for the first time since I could remember. It was the first time in years that I had seen her teeth like that. She looked like a normal happy girl on a winter day getting ready to go home and have a snowball fight with her family.

Our hands squeezed tighter together while Fawna and her friend whispered more about the plan. Freedom was a hop, skip, and a jump away and I almost couldn't contain myself.

Fawna's friend reiterated that when we got on the bus we should not look at the bus driver. We should keep our heads down and go right to the back and find as soon as possible. I was getting really nervous but had no time to collect myself and calm down. I was squeezing Camai's hand so tight. I let go as we approached to board. The big yellow bus hovered over me. My euphoria was changing to anxiety and distress. There was no turning back now. It was too late to return home. There was no way I was going back now, not with all my bags packed and my two sisters right at my side.

Camai went first. I followed the back of her feet up the big black steps. The bus gave off a heat and a smell that I will never forget. My heart couldn't have been beating any faster. I couldn't control it. I took a slow, deep breath and closed my eyes for a quick second. I envisioned our life hours from now, all sitting together around a small fire, with nothing but triumph and smiles. We can do this. We will survive.

I kept my eyes on the rubber strip and kept walking. Camai sat down in a seat right away but I had to keep walking because there wasn't a seat for me anywhere around her. I walked through many kids. They were all yelling and bouncing around the bus. I was scared because there were so many big kids. They were giving me dirty looks. My big duffel bag filled with cans and clothes barely fit through the aisle and I bumped many of the kids with it. Could I possibly have drawn any more attention to myself?

I continued to plow through kids and bags, so eager to sit down as soon as possible. Finally I caught sight of an open seat and plopped down immediately. I put my head on the seat in front of me. My breathing was fast and shallow as my heart beat uncontrollably. My hands trembled, so by instinct I shoved them under my legs like I was sitting on The Green Chair.

Fawna and her friend continued past me and found a seat in the very back. I hugged my bags on my lap and prayed we could just pull away from the school at that very moment. More kids were piling on as the bus waited and spewed out more of that putrid—yet promising—smell. The fumes from the bus exhaust seemed to be filling the inside. My chest felt heavy and my heartbeat almost came to a complete stop. Soon my stomach felt like a lead ball and I couldn't escape the bad feeling now consuming me.

I glanced up just enough to see over the top of the seats where Camai was sitting. She had her head down just like I did. I could see her beautiful shiny brown hair. I just wanted to be next to her. I saw all the other kids snickering and whispering among themselves. I quickly thought, "Just wait, everyone. In a few days, I'm going to be just as happy as you." In the corner of my eye I caught a glimpse I'll never be able to drive out of my memory. I saw the bus driver glaring at me. She had her radio up to her mouth and she was staring at me. I'll never forget that feeling as the pit in my stomach grew.

That's when it happened.

I quickly snapped my head down and started to panic. "Oh my God, she knows. She knows we aren't supposed to be on the bus." I jerked my head around to find Fawna. She was sitting a few seats behind me and I could tell something was wrong. She signaled me to be quiet and remained perked up, keeping aware of what was going on. Camai stayed curled up behind the seat the whole time. I was so proud of her. I wished I were sitting next to her, holding her hand. My heart was pounding in my chest so hard that I thought it was going to come out. I was breathing really fast. I looked up again and the bus driver was still staring at me and talking on her radio. I was beyond terrified.

After what seemed like an eternity, all the other buses drove away. We were the only bus left in the lot. The other kids on board were growing impatient, demanding to drive away too. Everything was in slow motion. I knew at that moment we were going home that night.

The other kids were bobbing up and down. They were screaming things at the bus driver. I just continued to look forward. I took some deep breaths and said a prayer. I never prayed to God before like I did at that instant. I prayed this was a dream. I wanted to be in that shed more than anything. I wanted to be off this bus, the bus driver to stop looking at me and to just drive away. God must have hated me.

Our principal stepped onto the bus a few moments later and stood tall at the front. All the kids became completely quiet and sat down right away. He didn't even need the speaker-phone for everyone to hear him. He had a concerned look on his face. I knew our plan had failed. He cleared his throat and bellowed loudly, "Can I have the three Millwood girls get off the bus and come with me please." He didn't seem mad, just worried. I didn't know what was going to happen. I just didn't want to go home that night.

Tears poured out of my eyes before I knew it. Camai didn't move. I looked back to see Fawna stand up first and start excusing herself through the pile of kids. She walked by my seat and said, "Come on, Jas, let's go. Everything's going to be okay."

I couldn't believe we didn't drive away. How did the bus driver know we didn't belong on the bus? I hated her. I stood up and grabbed my bags. I followed Fawna to the front. When I passed Camai I squeezed her arm lightly. She looked up at me with tears in her eyes. She was still grasping her bags like it was her life. Her lips began to tremble as she asked, "We didn't make it, did we?" I shook my head as tears flooded my eyes and dripped onto my clothes. I felt so bad to let her down. She had more hope than any of us. I cried because I had let my sisters down. I could only think this was my fault. My teacher knew I was lying and figured out the whole thing. I will never be able to forgive myself.

The walk to the principal's office took what felt like years. I was ashamed and embarrassed but I tried to remain strong. I never let go of Camai's hand. We walked off the bus. All the kids were screaming at us because we made them wait so long. They even threw something at us. I didn't care. It was nothing compared to what would happen when we got home.

When we finally got into the principal's office he had us all sit around a big wooden table. We set our bags down and sat in these chairs that had wheels on them. At first I was amused but after I realized the circumstances I began to cry again. He was so confused and didn't know what to say. My sisters and I kept looking at each other. The tears never stopped.

"Girls. What is wrong?" He asked. We continued to sob and couldn't even begin to get any words out. "Why are you crying? You girls need to explain to me what is going on—why were you on that bus today?" he said. My stomach was churning. I felt like I was going to throw up. I wanted to throw up. I didn't have anything in my stomach to throw up. Fawna just looked at the floor the whole time. The principal's secretary came into the room and offered us water and tissues.

"Girls. Calm down please. I need you to tell me why you got on that bus after school today. We are not leaving until you tell me what you were planning on doing."

All I could think about now was how Diane was at home, upset that we weren't home on time for her to grab us and throw us around as soon as we came inside. I knew she was getting angrier by the second and would probably start to look for us soon. Maybe it was a good idea to start talking. I looked over at my sisters again and could tell that they agreed. We sat up in our chairs, calmed down a little and started to talk.

We told him everything. We told him about all the abuse, the neglect, how we barely ate anything. We told him about Diane and how we were afraid of her. We just spilled it. We talked for an hour about everything. We showed him our bruises and welts. We even told him every detail of our runaway plan. We opened our bags and showed him everything we had packed so we could survive in the shed. He didn't say one word the entire time. He just sat there at his desk, just listening. He barely expressed any emotion or changed his facial expression, just continued to sit there in awe and disbelief.

But eventually the principal started to look suspicious. He knew us only as "trouble kids." He had been told that we lie and steal. When I began to sense that maybe he didn't believe us, we told him even more. I could tell he wanted to see proof that they spanked and whipped us. Cam stood up and pulled her pants down. She turned around and showed him her bottom. It was bruised and welted. She was crying and I could tell she was so ashamed. I was so proud of her for being brave.

The principal called in his secretary and asked for paperwork to create accident reports. She immediately returned with them. He also asked for some phone numbers and that she needed to send an email off to the school social worker.

I began to think this was going to be the end. I was thinking, "He knows. He won't send us home. Now everyone is going to know. We are finally going to be free! We should have just done this in the beginning!"

The principal sat up in his chair and ran his hands through his hair. He took a deep breath. He told us to go have a seat in the hallway while he took care of some things. We waited another twenty minutes outside his office. We were holding hands and crying. We whispered about not going home. We said that if by chance we were sent home that night, we would try again to run away. I wasn't going home. Not after this. For sure Diane would kill us. Dad would help her, too. We were scared and frustrated. I was confused and didn't know what was going to happen. This was twenty minutes my heart will never forget.

Finally the principal called us back into his office. He seemed overwhelmed. I could tell he didn't want to say what he was about to.

"Girls, I called your father and Diane. They are on their way to pick you up."

My heart sunk to the floor. I felt as if two-ton weights had just dropped onto my shoulders. I felt as if I were suffocating. I looked over to Cam as tears were flowing from her sad eyes. She was so scared; I could see her shaking. There is no way we are going back there. We are going to die tonight. Does he know we won't be in school tomorrow? Does he realize this is the last time he is going to see us if we go home with them?

"Don't be scared. Everything is going to be fine. You are a great family and are going to work this out."

Work this out? What the hell are you talking about? I'm going to be dead by the morning, I thought to myself. My sisters cried harder than we ever had before. I felt sick to my stomach. I started hyperventilating. The principal told us to grab all of our things and start walking outside. I scooted off the chair and wiped my face off. I leaned down and grabbed my two bags. They seemed so much heavier than they did this morning. I hauled them over my shoulder as I walked with my sisters toward the outside doors.

It had begun to snow again. It seemed even colder than earlier. I couldn't stop myself from shaking or even control my breathing. I kept telling myself to stop crying but I couldn't help it. The tears just kept falling down my cheeks onto the ice-covered pavement.

In the parking lot, the principal told us to wait and that our parents would be here any minute. Before we knew it dad and Diane flew into the parking lot and around the bend and loudly jolted to a quick stop. Diane was glaring at me through the windshield. There was no turning back now.

The doors opened at the same time and they came running out. Diane ran up to Camai flailing her arms and hugged her dramatically.

"Why would you girls do something like this? You know that we love you! We are a great family; you don't even want to give us a chance?" Diane sobbed. She even had a tear on her cheek. I didn't know she was capable of such an emotion.

What a load of crap. Are you kidding me? Are you really pretending like you are a perfect parent? This can't be real. You can't possibly be putting on this show. But then again, she had perfected the act of the non-accepted stepmother victim very well—this was probably a piece of cake.

In no time my father had taken all of our bags from us and put them in the trunk. He looked so embarrassed. He wasn't putting on an act like Diane, though. He just thanked the principal for taking care of us and making sure we were safe.

They didn't say much more until we piled into the backseat. They thanked the prinicpal for "finding us" ad taking care of us. Diane continued her little performance and sniffled as she climbed back into the car. I could tell my dad was disappointed and didn't know what to say. The car doors were slammed shut and we were headed home. I looked through the window and saw the principal standing there. He had a fake smile plastered on his face. I knew he believed us. So then why did he send us home? Snowflakes were falling on his black suit coat. His nose was red and he was rubbing his hands together to stay warm but he just stood there. I watched him all the way until we left the parking lot. I couldn't believe he made us go back. I hated him.

Nobody said one word the whole two minutes home. It was such a loud silence. I was surprised; I expected Diane to turn around, climb over the seats, and batter us until we were all in a coma. She had stopped crying, of course, but remained silent. You could tell my father was extremely upset. He was speechless. His eyes seemed glazed over but he wasn't crying.

After we pulled into the driveway we all got out of the car. Fawna went to get her bags but Ben instructed us that he would take care of everything. We walked into the house slowly. Diane didn't even follow us. One by one we entered the house. It smelled different. Something wasn't right. I had a bad feeling about what was about to happen.

We quickly scattered to our own rooms and waited patiently. Every minute felt like an hour. All I kept thinking about was how we didn't make it. We were so close—inches away from freedom. I kept playing it over and over in my head. I tried to pinpoint the exact reason we got caught. Questions flooded my mind. I just kept thinking it was me. The bus driver saw me. I was the reason we got caught. My sisters would never forgive me. They will never speak to me again. I cried for a while and rocked back and forth, praying for a painless night. That was my way of coping with things; I rocked back and forth like a little toddler on a rocking chair with my mommy. It wasn't loud and it comforted me. It made me feel safe. I felt untouchable. But nothing was untouchable to Diane.

It was dark before I knew it. I heard dad and Diane talk a couple of times. Their voices were muffled but the tone just didn't sound good. I was so scared. A part of me wanted to be killed that night. I just wanted Diane to kill me. Get it over with. Then our principal and bus driver would have learned their lesson. They would feel so guilty. I just wanted to die, not only for that reason. I would rather be dead than have to go through the pain of living here another day.

I shivered in my room when I heard a knock at the front door. It startled me so I perked up and tried to listen. At first dad and Diane weren't going to answer it. But the person at the door persisted. Whoever it was knew we were home. Who could it be? Who knocks on our door at this time of night?

I heard the front door swing open slowly. Dad and Diane warmly greeted the person and went on talking in a pleasant manner.

Maybe it was a relative? Perhaps a social worker? Questions that could be answered only by my own eyes.

I knew we wouldn't be allowed to come out. Whoever it was, dad and Diane probably told them that we had been bad all day and weren't allowed to visit with company. I tried to listen closely and heard our names a couple times. It sounded like there were maybe two or three visitors, right outside my room. One of the voices sounded familiar but I couldn't quite figure out who it may be.

After 15 minutes or so, Diane tapped lightly on my door. I sat straight up and looked at her when she entered. She flicked the light switch on and came and sat by my bed. She seemed relaxed and content. I was confused and now very apprehensive.

"Jasmine honey, there are some people in the living room who want to see you. Go out there and be very polite. Remember what I told you about telling strangers things about your family?"

"What the hell is going on?" I screamed in my head. "Is this a joke? You've got to be kidding me, right? This isn't real. Diane is putting on another one of her acts!" But I nodded and walked out into the living room. To my surprise I saw my teacher from school and two other adults I didn't recognize. I couldn't believe it. Is this a miracle?

I sat down on the sofa and hung my head low. I didn't know what to do. After everything that had happened today I tried to not be too open. I remained guarded. My teacher came closer to me and put her arm around my back. Her touch was warm and gentle and it was the safest I had ever felt in this home. I felt a tug-of-war in my heart as I wanted to hug her but still obey Diane. I felt uneasy but for some reason happy. Her soft face and big white teeth sparkled despite the implications of the situation. I could tell she was uncomfortable and unsatisfied. I looked her square in the eyes and knew in my heart she could tell I needed her to help my sisters and me. She was a little chubbier than our other teachers and I remember daydreaming for a second, thinking how I wanted to snuggle up into her arms and let her carry me away at this exact moment.

The teachers started asking me things about dad and Diane. I wanted to tell them everything. But I remembered what Diane told me, so I kept my mouth shut. I was smart enough not to slip. I told them that I loved Diane and she was a really good stepmom, that they never did anything to hurt us. I reassured them that I was very happy there.

The teachers quietly sat there for a moment. The silence was palpable. They all looked at each other, and then back at me.

My teacher gave a big sigh and scooted closer to me. Then she knelt down in front of me and put her hands on my shoulders. She looked me square in the eyes and said, "Sweetie...if you are so happy here, then why did you try to run away?"

My eyes instantaneously welled up with tears. I was speechless. Diane hadn't told me what to say to a question like this. I started to panic. I looked around at their faces. They, too, began to cry. The other adult wiped her eyes and wrote something down on some paper. I lowered my head and took some deep breaths. I was in for it. There was no way in hell I could attempt to run away and give it away to my teachers all in one day without getting it bad.

I stood up and my teacher gave me a hug. She was more determined than the other adults and teachers and I felt like she wouldn't let me down. She squeezed me so hard that I couldn't breathe for a second. After she let go she turned around and sat back down on the sofa as I returned to my bunk bed in my room. I had never been in a situation like this. Diane was going to kill me. But then I remembered, I wanted to die.

I still couldn't believe the teachers came to our house. What were they doing here? I remembered leaving the school parking lot in my dad's car and looking at the principal, begging him with my eyes to rescue us. The look in his eyes was reassuring. He must have told our teachers what happened. They all probably conferred with each other what they had noticed. Maybe this was the beginning of the end.

After our teachers left, Cam came back in our room and we climbed into bed. Diane is probably going to kill us in our sleep. This would be the night. A knife? A fire? What would the murder scene look like?

Despite the events of the day, I drifted off into a light sleep. That night I dreamed about my Uncle Richard. I wondered what wondered if he thought about us often. I was thinking about his ice cream with cereal on top and how we were allowed to watch cartoons. I dreamed he took my sisters and me to the zoo and we had a great time seeing all the animals and running around. In my dream he let us have a lollipop (which was so unlike him) and we were so happy, so healthy, so normal.

I wondered what he would think upon learning of our scheme to run away. Would he be mad? Would he understand why we did it? I missed him. I would have given anything to live with him again.

Turning Point 10

To my surprise, we woke up the next morning. I didn't know what emotion to feel. I was exhausted and starving but afraid to even move. My dad came in sometime very early and demanded I go apologize to Diane. He kneeled down and grabbed me by my arms, looked me straight in the eyes, and said, "Diane is extremely hurt you tried to run away. You owe her an apology for acting up and not respecting her."

I listened, of course. I left my room and walked slowly downstairs where she was folding laundry. I slowly crept down the stairs and walked up to her. I wasn't sure exactly what to say but I knew I had better say it fast. She never looked at me. I just watched her fold clothes for a minute until I started my request for forgiveness.

"Diane... I'm really sorry... for trying to run away. I will start respecting you more. I am sorry for ruining your life."

She didn't even acknowledge my presence. She didn't even look at me. She pretended that it bothered her that we tried to run away by sniffling and shooing me away but I didn't fall for it. She was probably only scared because our teachers came to our house that night and this might actually develop into something. She could go to jail for what she has done. But she seemed to believe, deep down, that we would never be able to tell the truth about what happened in this home.

I turned around and headed back upstairs. I had a small smile on my face as I climbed the stairs. I realized at this moment, as I left that cold, moldy basement where my abuser stood, that we had lost every battle in this conflict but we had won the war. Our courage and bravery had finally paid off. The only question now was how much longer were we going to have to stay here? And what was she going to do the next time she had us alone?

The morning continued as usual; Diane had our chores all set up. We had 45 minutes to clean the entire house. I cleaned the kitchen, Cam did the bathroom and Fawna did everything else. I was even more exhausted than before and hungrier than ever. Diane screamed at us to finish everything before school or we would regret it. I was rushing but didn't want to miss anything in case she was in the mood for violence.

After we went to school that morning my teacher's attitude had completely changed. Instead of her usual behavior where she judged me about the lunchbox raid, she brought me a lunch. It had a sandwich, apple, Cheetos, a granola bar, and a Capri Sun in it. She told me I didn't have to do any of the schoolwork if I didn't want to. If I needed to talk or even leave the room I had permission to do so.

I could tell that she was really being compassionate and truly cared about my safety. She was a smart woman. Not just because she fed me or made sure I was treated like a princess now during school hours but because she knew. She knew deep down at least some of what I went through when I went home after school. She believed my sisters and me. The first of only a few people to ever *act*. We never talked about it but I knew something was different. The nurse started taking us out of class once or twice a week. Then it turned to once a day. She wrote down every bruise and mark on my body. She examined my skull that was hardly healing. She said she could feel the scar tissue and asked if I ever got headaches. She knew I was lucky to be alive.

Social workers began to show up at the house more frequently with more serious visits. We began talking to them alone more often, too. They seemed to be listening more intently and writing down what we said. I was rude to them only because they didn't believe us in the first place. I still continued to lie about the abuse, either by instinct or because they had already let us down so many times before.

My sisters and I whispered on the way to school about the visits because we all could feel something was different. We never talked about what to say, so I just assumed we would keep doing what we had been doing the last two years. I think we knew that until we were actually physically removed from the home we couldn't put ourselves in more harm.

I could tell the social workers were putting together pieces of the puzzle, but were never smart enough to take us the day they came to visit. And after every day they left Diane made sure she gave us a piece of the pie we had been missing.

"You little shits! You think you're going to get out of here but you won't! They would have taken you by now!" she would scream. We pretended to believe her but I knew it was only a matter of time. Her whips and kicks hurt more than ever but she wasn't tearing down my pride anymore. She hit us with more force and beat us using more power but my heart was still beating.

The last few months we were there were the worst. Since the day we had tried to run away we figured it wouldn't be long, but months went by and we were still there. It was getting warmer and we were growing more exhausted and less hopeful. Diane continued to find the most obnoxious ways to harm us. She banged me up against the stove and threw me on the floor to jump on me. She pulled my hair out and threw bleach on my skin. My sisters, too. She knew the end was coming. She would soon have no one to hurt and take her anger out on. She would have nobody to make herself feel better. Everyone would know what she did to us. Maybe not until years later, but sooner or later everyone was bound to find out. She was a criminal.

Social workers began to show up almost every day and I noticed their attitude toward Diane had now changed. Instead of being her friend, they treated her in a civil manner but disregarded anything that came out of her mouth. They started saying things about moving. They even told us to think about who we would want to live with if we were to leave dad and Diane. I still believed Diane when she told us nobody wanted us, so I never gave them an answer. Part of me also didn't believe them when they asked me that question. Diane would act so happy and polite when they arrived and turned into a monster when they left. She told them we were such a happy family and that we all got along great. Finally the social workers had stopped believing her. They were finally on our side. This just enraged Diane even more. There was nothing she could do about what was going to happen.

My sisters and I finished school that year. Poor Fawna didn't even get to go to her fifth-grade graduation. Diane made her eat this cold pasta salad dish that Fawna didn't like. It was little things like that that really got to us. All the beatings and screaming didn't matter because they were so frequent and severe we had become numb to them. What mattered was that I couldn't be a ladybug in the school play or Fawna couldn't attend her own fifth-grade graduation ceremony. Or that Cam truly believed she was a disgusting pig. Those are the things that got to us. Diane used every last minute with us to bring us down as much as she could.

The following text has been directly copied from official case documents written by a social worker during the last few months in the home and following the removal. I believe the implications this excerpt from my file has on the allegations described in this book are profound.

From the service plan dating from the period 2/4/97 to 4/4/1997:

During the last part of this quarter Mr. Millwood and the children stopped attending counseling. They indicated that the counseling did not appear to be making a difference and that they were financially unable to continue attending. All three girls indicated they did not wish to continue counseling, also. That was their position before the counseling began. Mr. Millwood was not in agreement with taking the children to counseling either. The family attended in order to comply with the court order. While financial concerns are realistic, they were probably not overriding the factor in the families withdrawal, as the Agency was picking up the majority of the cost. It seems likely that Mr. Millwood became increasingly disillusioned with the treatment progress as both Dr. (Unnamed) and the worker attempted to use it for what it was designed to do, effect some type of stabilization in the home and between the birth mother and the children. Any move towards reconciliation with the birth mother was strongly resisted and resented by Mr. Millwood.

Mr. Millwood indicated by phone that girls behavior was difficult but tolerable in the home and he had no further plans to re-attend therapy.

In the last quarter the worker has observed the father, stepmother, and children in the home. Overall there is a surface layer of calm and organization. The home is consistently clean, the kitchen spotless, the girls' shoes arranged neatly on the floor in the back hall. There is a sense of military precision. There is also a strong structure to the day. There are discussions where the family discusses what it means to be a family. The children appear to respond well to parental directives. Some corporal punishment does go on, but it is infrequent, light by all accounts, and administered for reasons that appear to fall within cultural norms.

But below the surface, there is a strong undercurrent of psychological warfare, hostility, and unreasonable expectations on the part of Mr. Millwood and Diane. The girls seems to be willing adversaries in the conflict: it is the girls versus Ben and Diane. For example, if the girls shoes are out of line in the back hall by a few inches, the parents feel compelled to make an intervention into this "resistant" behavior. If the girls moan when it is time to come inside from playing in the backyard, they are "breaking the rules." Neither parent appears to have the ability to accept normal developmental behavior on the girls' part as anything other than behavioral pathology that requires immediate intervention and eradication.

At this point, the three girls have bought into this system. I do not believe they fell into organized resistance to it in the first year and half of placement. They worked very hard to comply with expectations; they wanted to be a family unit. But the unbending expectations of the parents have worn them down. They are now united as a unit, whispering, conspiracies, manipulations against the parents.

At the same time this family is in a war with itself, it is closed off from the outside world. Intrusions by outsides—even those potentially helpful ones who may be able to alleviate the pain within the family—are resented and resisted. There is the same sense of resistant isolation that is felt when working with spousal abuse couples: the situation is terrible but they are unlikely to allow or change a separation from each other.

The driving force in all of this is probably the stepmother, Diane (Unnamed), as she and the father married during this quarter. Diane indicates that she was raise by an abusive bi-polar father. This appears to have had a considerable impact on her. For example, any conversation with her related to the children and parenting techniques results—within a few minutes—to her telling stories about how she was raised, which included her father hitting her with boards.

To a large extent Diane justifies her father's behavior and identifies with him as the aggressor, "I was hit with boards, and look at me, I turned out alright." She is not emotionally able to look at her own father's behavior as truly inappropriate or to fully express the anger and resentment she feels related to his treatment of her.

This has left her incapable of understanding that it is not appropriate to apply those same techniques with the Millwood girls. At this point she does not engage in the extreme corporal punishment of the girls, but the more subtle aspects of the psychological abuse she must have undergone are played out on daily basis, including unreasonable expectations and emotional blackmail.

At the same time, Diane refuses to view the problem as one that she has a responsibility for creating and maintaining. She thinks the girls have problems, someone needs to "fix" the girls. Sure, she was hit with boards, but she's alright.

One goal of the therapy was to subtly induct Dawn into a therapeutic milieu to see if she could respond appropriately and make any gains from the process. Her primary mechanism for maintaining her distance from the therapist was to manipulate Ben from the sidelines and get him to view the therapy as unproductive. This manipulation was readily evident during the worker home visits this quarter. Mr. Millwood would be talking and Diane would lean over and whisper someone in his ear. Mr. Millwood would immediately appear conflicted and change his position. This would happen two or three times in the middle of an hour long conversation. Additionally, Diane would preface her verbal statements with phrases such as, "But Ben, don't you think that," or "You know that's not..." The tone is steady, plaintive, cajoling: "Come on Ben, you know that..." She holds his hand, makes eye contact.

Mr. Millwood has been helpless in this game. He has been steadily pulled into the orbit of a much stronger, more psychologically disturbed person, Diane. He is not able to sort through these issues or examine his personal commitments or responsibilities except through Diane's eyes. And Diane, of course, has her own agenda and, as has always been expected, her ultimate agenda probably consists of three sequential steps: Marry Mr. Millwood; get rid of the girls; have a child of her own. There is a very strong sense of inevitability to this plan, a true script. The Millwood family is no longer about Ben or the three Millwood girls; it is about Diane.

Child Protective Services in Livingston County became involved with the family during this quarter as the result of an incident involving corporal punishment by Ben against one of the girls. Both the FLA Worker and PS Worker believe this incident did occur and agreed to open a prevention case. The PS worker has indicated in letters to the family that he may remove the girls if Mr. Millwood does not comply with the intensive services offered by the prevention.

At this time, it is unclear whether Mr. Millwood will accept these services into his home. The worker reiterated that he must comply with Livingston County or it will have serious repercussions related to the placement of his children.

In reality, it is questionable whether or not this process will be successful. They key, again, is Diane. She will most certainly view the presence of intensive in-home services in her home as a threat to her own defense system, and I believe it is unlikely she will engage in it.

Furthermore, the Agency has arranged for worker supervised visitation with the biological mother, but the father has been extremely uncooperative and will not transport the children to any location.

From the service plan dating from the period 4/5/97 to 7/5/1997:

At present, all three children are placed with relatives. The father had begun to request removal in late May, 1997, and they were eventually removed at the end of June, 1997, following the June 18, 1997 court order from which DHS obtained an order to remove.

The father has indicated that the girls are too much for him and he now wishes to have them placed back into foster care. He is able to state specific problems that he has with the girls, including lying and stealing, but at the same time consistently refuses any help that may assist him. He has been given a blank check to services in Livingston County while refusing to engage but at the same time complaining about the girls' behavior.

The father and stepmother's expectations for the children were consistently unrealistic across the life of the placement. The specifically state that they, "Don't give any love back to us," and that "they are not growing emotionally," and that these are the reasons they should be removed. They further state they need to be put somewhere that "they can get the help they need."

The parents appeared to have had little understanding of what constituted developmentally appropriate needs and behavior on the girls' part, but at the same time were closed to all efforts related to instruction or counseling. In the end, it was Ben's way (which is really Diane's way), or else get out.

The Great Rescue 11

I walked down the five crooked steps and took a deep breath. I didn't know exactly what was going on but the morning had started off unlike the usual. My blood was hot as it raced through the veins in my body but I held my head high with everything I had. I looked forward, afraid to believe what my eyes were seeing. I looked to my sisters for support, but they were just as scared and confused as I was. Fawna looked perplexed yet angry. The social workers told us nothing. Nobody told us anything. There was a U-haul truck backed up in our gravel driveway. Familiar faces stood staggered all around. Was this a dream?

Most of the faces triggered a flashback of smiles and great memories from earlier in my life; things I no longer knew of. I felt like I couldn't breathe. I looked back at my father and silently requested his approval to continue. He just looked over to *her* and then down to the grass. My lungs were gasping for air and my body was fully tense. I felt that if I stopped moving forward I would get stuck. The faces of people we had seen so little of in the last two years looked appalled. Many of them were crying and turned away. I thought to myself, I must be that ugly that they can't even look at me. I was so confused. I was even more scared. What does this mean? What is going on?

When I finally made it down the steps, a social worker came up to me and softly grabbed my hand. She led me over to a tall grey-haired man standing near the back end of the U-haul. She leaned over and whispered in a gentle voice, "Jasmine, this is your Uncle Richard, do you remember your Uncle Richard?"

My lips started to tremble and my mind flooded with memories of a different life, memories I had erased long ago. I could smell his scent of lotion and home-cooked meals. My uncle always kept us safe and gave us clothes and food. The last time I remember talking to him was about a year and a half ago, when we were still allowed to talk on the phone. I remember he asked me if I had any mosquito bites and I was so happy to be able to count all of them for him. I remember being happy he was keeping me on the phone as long as possible. I remember secretly wishing he would ask me if I had any bruises, but I would never be able to tell him the truth even if he did.

Uncle Richard leaned over and put his hands out to take my belongings. I handed him a box with everything I owned. How pathetic, a cardboard box with all of my possessions. I remembered him vividly but part of me didn't want to. I couldn't look him in the eyes. I was too afraid that *she* would get mad. I couldn't possibly think that we were lucky enough to actually escape from this horrible nightmare.

Uncle Richard took my box and put it in the bottom of the truck. I pushed my sleeve up and wiped away the tears falling down my cheeks. I didn't even know what was happening but I felt uneasy and terrified. All I could think about is, if we leave, when we come back we are going to die. She always told us that if we ever said anything to anyone, that she would kill us. I began to fear that exact moment. But when I looked over at her, she seemed so calm, yet giddy. I started to consider the possibility that we were actually leaving, and realized she was probably smiling because she was finally getting my father all to herself. I began to feel very sick.

The social worker then took my hand again and led me over to more of those faces. I couldn't find it in myself to gather enough courage to look at them in their eyes. My dad stood silently by the house with his arms crossed, looking down at the ground. Coward. I could tell he was crying and wondered if he was sad that he would never see us again or that people had finally found out what they had done.

A few minutes passed while people loaded our belongings into the truck. They put three bikes, three boxes and some furniture inside. Some of these things we hadn't seen since we arrived. My sisters and I stood close together, clenching each other's hands and whispering rumors about freedom. All of the people gathered and whispered more. Most of them stood there in awe and disbelief that these were the same three girls that they had last seen two years ago. The anticipation was climbing and soon everything became blurry. I held my twin Camai's hand tightly as we tried to figure out what was going on. We were crying but didn't know why. Was this just for one night? Or forever?

The possibility that we might be separated could be devastating to each of us and cause irreparable trauma. There is no way you can take me away from my sisters. Never again we will be alone in this world, not after what we just went through. We have learned to stick together and nothing will bring us apart. I continue to clench Cam's hand as hard as I can in case they begin to tear us apart.

It was when the clouds rolled in and the U-haul truck door slammed shut that I knew. Freedom. These familiar faces are our rescuers. They have finally found us and they have finally come to save us. This is it—this is goodbye!

Since this is goodbye I know what is next. We have to *say* goodbye. Someone is behind me, nudging me toward them. I never dreaded anything more in my life. I walk up to her first. I move close to her and look her in her eyes. Goosebumps graze my frail skin but I feel even hotter than before. It takes every ounce of courage and bravery in me but I do it. I am shaking tremendously but I know she won't touch me in front of all these people. I move a few more inches near her. My arms are so heavy; I can't lift them and I absolutely don't want to touch her. I can't bring myself to do it. The amount of nervous energy is increasing by the second. Why is this so hard? I am saying goodbye!

She leans her arms over me and wraps them around me. I flinch when she moves, but all I really want is for this hug from hell to be over. Her hug feels like pure hatred—as if I am screaming as loud as I can but nobody can hear me. I can smell her coffee breath and see her dry skin. Her scraggly hair covers my face as I hold my breath. She is putting on a great show for the audience. Making them all believe she is a loving stepmother who actually cares for us. What a lie.

After what seems like an eternity, I quickly back away, as far away from her as possible. I don't say even one word to her. I feel a sense of relief but I learned years prior to this day to never own any sense of hope. Hope was not something I knew of. Hope was nonexistent in the lives of my sisters and me.

Then I walk over to my dad. That was six feet I will never forget. My hands are trembling and I stop breathing altogether. The only thing I can focus on is my tiny feet with each step on the patchy grass. I didn't want to leave him. He loved us. I still wanted to be daddy's little girl. I wanted one last daddy-daughter dance with him. I wanted to have picnics and Christmas together. I say to myself, *she* was the one who hurt us *most* of the time. You only did it when she told you to. I always wanted to believe these two years were all a nightmare. I wished I would wake up and it would all be over. But the part of him I kept inside my heart was dying. I had to let go.

I stand in front of him as he towers over me. I look down at the grass and dandelions and pray that this moment isn't real. My dad kneels down and I look him in the eyes. His beautiful green eyes. The eyes he gave me. He puts his big hand on my shoulder. It is warm and filled with a kind touch. I feel so safe at this moment because I begin to realize that she would never hurt me again. He starts to speak and tears well up in my eyes. I can't see him anymore so I just listen to his deep voice.

"You'll always be my little princess," he says.

"I love you, daddy. I don't want to go," I beg. "I promise I won't be bad anymore. Please don't make me go. I love you."

I didn't realize it at that time but I was pleading for my own father's support and approval and he would never, in my whole life, give that to me.

He wipes the tears from my eyes with his calloused hand and says, "Jasmine honey, you have to go. Uncle Richard will take care of you. Everything will be fine. Just be a good little girl and everything will be fine."

And that is it. He wraps his strong arms around me and squeezes tightly. Then he lets go and turns me to the faces. I feel his warm hands resting on my shoulders and I take a deep breath. I walk away from him thinking deep down we would be back tomorrow. That we would wake up on our hard mattresses and take a few bites of the awful puffed wheat cereal and do our chores. None of this seems real. This is all just an imagination. I must be dreaming somewhere while lying unconscious waiting to wake up from the last beating. But I have a slight smile on my face because I truly believe that someday I will be daddy's little princess again. Little do I know that that eerie

June morning would be the one of the last times I would ever see him again.

The people with the familiar faces had to carry Fawna to our car. She was hysterical and screaming. I don't remember why she was acting this way. Maybe it was because she thought we would came back and get it worse than we ever got it before. She always tried to protect us the best she could. I think she was trying to send some sort of message to the people taking us away—that when we came back we were going to die. She always had the most courage of all of us. But at this moment she was the weakest. She could barely even walk. She sobbed so loudly and I could feel her pain deep in my soul.

Uncle Richard hopped into the U-haul and drove away. Cam and I went into the backseat of our Aunt Debbie's car. Fawna was practically hyperventilating in the front seat while Aunt Debbie was trying to calm her down. My Aunt Debbie kept repeating, "Only happy tears from now on," over and over. Her warm voice soothed my feeling of unease. I kept my eyes shut as I thought about what my gravestone would say: "Here lies Jasmine, one of three sisters who were murdered by a woman with no soul. Let them Rest in Peace, Finally." I truly believed in my heart we would be back. And she would kill us. We drove off in the cloudy but eerily calm afternoon. I just listened to my aunt's voice and let it soothe my uneasy soul.

After I was able to regain enough strength to hold back any more tears, I wiped them away I looked up into the window and saw my reflection. It was in that moment I understood why the faces had looked so appalled when they first saw me. I first noticed the bony structure and then my thin, colorless flesh. Then I saw big, dark circles under my eyes. I had no energy, no life, no motivation. I looked completely empty. I was mentally and physically drained from two years in a prison.

I picked up my arm and stared at my bones as they seemed to protrude out of my skin. There were burn scars, cuts, scrapes, and bruises covering me. I couldn't believe what I looked like. I was so ugly. How could anybody ever care about someone who looks so ugly? How could anyone ever love someone so hideous? I tried to ignore my appearance. Then, suddenly, I realized that it didn't matter what we looked like—my sisters and I made it out alive. We escaped. We had been starved, tortured and nearly beaten to death every day for two years. It was finally the end. When I realized this I put my head in my hands and began to silently sob. It was something I learned to do when I didn't want her to hear me crying. I would weep for hours without making a sound. I sat there in the backseat, head in my hands, and just cried. Crying for relief, for freedom, for my life, for my sisters.

We headed straight to my Aunt Debbie's house. On the way there the sun broke through the clouds and I felt a warmth come over me in the backseat of the car that I had never felt before. I looked over at Cam, who gave me a half smile. Fawna sat silent in the front seat with her head hanging low. I knew she understood something that I didn't. It would take years before I comprehended the implications this day had on our lives and the people we would become—both good and bad. My aunt just put her arm around her and stroked the back of her tiny blonde head.

During the last two years we were prohibited from any contact with any family member or person related to my mother, but my aunts and cousins often drove through the streets of Brighton looking for us. They searched almost every street, alley, and playground for my sisters and me. But we were very rarely outside. We were behind closed doors. We were away from anyone who could protect us. They weren't ever going to find us; at least that's what I always thought.

My Aunt Debbie invited many of my family members over to see us for the first time since we moved away. She ordered pizza and had my sisters and me sit down around the table. People came in I did not recognize. Many of my cousins cried when they saw us. They covered their mouths with their hands and turned around in shock. We just weren't the same three little girls. They couldn't believe what we looked like. People came up to us and gave us big hugs. There were people everywhere crying, laughing, and staring. I was extremely uncomfortable but thought anything was better than being back in that prison.

We devoured the pizza and other food. It was so delicious. My sisters and I ate until our stomachs couldn't hold any more. We were so grateful for the food. We must have said thank you about a hundred times. After hours of tears, conversations, and reuniting, my sisters and I split up. We each went home with a different aunt. We each found our way out that night, heads high, thinking and deeply hoping that we were going to find the happy childhood that was cut short two years ago.

Looking back at myself, on a personal level, at this time is heartbreaking. I lacked even a single bit of confidence. My dignity was so weak that nothing could bring me down—I was already as down as a person could be. I was too afraid to look anyone in his or her eyes. My body was fragile—not just physically but mentally. I weighed just 52 pounds and stood a mere 52 inches. I was ten years old but no heavier than a five-year-old. I was only bones and skin. My hands were calloused and red from constantly working with dangerous cleaning chemicals. My hair was brittle from two years of being thrown around and ripped out. My skin was bruised and scarred from the whippings and beatings. After leaving my dad's house, I knew only a few things. We had been brainwashed there, completely wiped out. We knew how to clean a house until there wasn't one speck of dirt. We knew how to take care of ourselves—nurse open wounds and take care of bruises. We knew how to look at the floor for hours at a time. We knew the best way to tense up while we were being kicked and punched. All of these things were our lives, the only things that were reality to us.

My sisters and I were separated for two weeks. I knew my sisters were safe but constantly asked my aunt to reassure me they weren't back with my dad. Those first two weeks were amazing. I slept pretty good that first night—in a warm bed with clean sheets. When I woke up that morning we ate a huge breakfast that my uncle cooked, full of pancakes, hash browns, and bacon. I felt as if this was all a dream. How could anyone love me so much to feed me, give me clothes, and hug me? Most of the food I started to eat was food I had never even smelled in years. I almost had to get used to it. I had stomach aches a lot after we moved out. We had to get used to getting vitamins and nutrients. Our stomachs had to get used to eating things like fat and starch. I learned it helped to eat little bites at a time. My body could now store food for energy, which was something all three of us had to get used to.

The first few days I was with my aunt, I didn't eat much at all. I would wake up and begin to do chores, starting with the bathroom. My aunt would wake up and yell at me and tell me to go watch some cartoons and eat a bowl of cereal. This was so hard to comprehend. It just didn't feel right. I felt like I had to walk on eggshells. I wanted to clean all day. I was afraid of everything. I thought if I did something bad I was going to go back there. This fear consumed my life.

After I finally believed that my sisters and I were truthfully given a second chance, I was able to begin to enjoy life and act like a normal little girl. Life became incredible those first few days out. I felt like a princess and that I was given another chance as a child to be happy. Little did I know of the difficult road that lay ahead. My fate included four years of night terrors and a lifetime of explaining to every new friend why I don't have a mom or dad. There were so many fluctuations in my physical appearance as I tried to define who I was without parents to guide me. I would hate the way I looked until I was 19. I would starve myself in attempts to "get skinny" for seven years. All sorts of problems were about to occur and I stood at the starting line of a long road to recovery.

It wasn't even the end of July before I began to remember the horrors and recount the memories. I would wake up in the middle of the night quivering because I could feel her presence in the room. I felt as if she was just waiting for me to wake up with a belt in hand and grin on her face.

I began to have night terrors in which I would wake up thinking she was standing over me with a knife. Nightmares began to occur every night, as I remembered all the ways Diane used to torture us. I remembered how she never let us wear summer clothes when it was blistering hot outside. She liked to have us wear things to torment us and make us extremely uncomfortable. My sisters and I played it off as if we didn't care, but every sweater and hideous dress with colored tights just tore us down even more. Every day that it seemed to get hotter, the heavier the sweaters and thicker the pants got. I remember during the second summer there I had this hot pink wool sweater that seemed to weigh more than I did. It had neon flowers on it that stuck out about an inch. It was so thick that I couldn't even scratch an itch. Diane knew that this sweater really got to me. I had to wear it for four days straight in the middle of July. The more kids made fun of us about the clothes we were forced to wear, the uglier the dresses and spandex pants got. It was as if she knew we were sweating to death under our bulky clothes or that we were being made fun of constantly at school. It was all just part of her plan.

One day while I was staying with my aunt, my cousins took me shopping. They bought me cute jean shorts and lacey tank tops that sparkled. They bought me barrettes for my hair and flip-flops that fit my feet. I was dressed up so nice like a little girl should be dressed on a hot summer day. Despite their generous attempt, on the inside I felt like an old woman, with no strength, confidence, or self-motivation.

I had scars and bruises that each told a specific story. Every time I looked down at them I relived that moment when I was terrified and fighting for my life. I was still scared to smile, scared to talk, even afraid to look people in their eyes. A huge part of me still felt as if I were in a dream. That I was going to wake up one day sore from yesterday's beatings, being dragged by my hair while she screamed her hot coffee-soaked breath down my neck.

I missed my sisters a lot during this time. I was so afraid they had gotten sent back—getting it worse because I had gotten out. I was still nervous about being away from them. I had just spent two years looking after them, just like they looked after me. I wanted to go back. Maybe Diane will change. I wouldn't be bad anymore…as long as my sisters were still alive. My sisters and I always stuck together. Being apart just killed me. Soon, though, that feeling began to diminish. I finally came to really believe what had changed.

On that muggy June morning we were free from Diane forever. God had answered our prayers and given us a miracle. He gave us a chance at a somewhat happy childhood. He put walking angels in our lives and smiles on our faces. He gave me hope, love, and energy back. Most importantly, he put someone in charge of saving our lives.

A few years later my father sent Fawna a letter. It rambled on for four or five pages. I was too young to understand it and have misplaced his letter since then but it sounded like a bunch of nonsense to me at the time. Things about doing what he had to do and how he didn't know how else to punish us for all the bad things we did. He explained he was terminating his own rights as a parent. This meant that he legally wasn't allowed to have any contact with us until our 18th birthdays. He chose to give up the three of us in order to live his own life. Terminating your own rights includes eliminating all financial responsibility. Ironic how one man cowardly runs away from the life and the choices he made and another man sacrifices everything to save three little girls who aren't even his own.

The email that I included in the beginning of this book helps serve as a reminder that my biological father chose Diane over us. Every time he sat there while she went on a violent rampage, he chose her. My only explanation is that he loved her more. She was what was more important to him. I still give him credit for the circumstances when we left that house that day. The social workers gave my father the choice to either continue to "care" for us or give us an opportunity to live in a different home. They asked my father if he wanted to keep us and I believe he made the first good decision in his life by letting us go. I want to believe he thought we deserved a better life and that he would never be able to provide that for us. I do believe he wanted what was best for me. I'm going to keep believing that, too, because it makes me feel good. I believe he wanted me to eat good food and play fun games. I believe he wanted me to twirl around like a princess and actually be one. My father knew deep down we would be better off. So he took those two years and put them in his pocket and waved goodbye. I never knew, until now, it was a goodbye that meant forever.

My big sister wrote the poem below about a year before graduating from high school. I didn't read it until five years later, when I stumbled upon it in one of her journals. I wept as I relived her pain for cutting off the relationship with my father and realized the sadness she lived with for her inability to protect her baby sisters. I felt proud she was able to write this poem and express these emotions. I feel proud that you are able to read her poem, too. I couldn't find better words to end this chapter.

Daddy I Love You

Daddy I love you, Daddy I need you
Daddy please don't go, don't go cause I love you
Daddy please don't leave us,
don't leave us in this cruel world without you

He gives her the one last hug
as he pulls away with his tear filled eyes.
As he whispers, "It's for the best, take care of them."
Her eyes were dry as daddy always said "Be strong."
Things she remembered as she buckled her seat belt.
Her Aunt drove South on I-275,
and the girl's heart and soul ached.

She could never before take care of them.
Daddy's hands always pushed bruises on little sisters
as they combed their thinning hair.
She never could take care of them

as step-mom used branches to cure lying little sisters.
As they cleaned bathroom sink with AJAX cleaner,
hoping the fumes would cause them to faint
And fall into another world far away
from the whipping of their back legs.

Silent tears fell from little sisters' faces,
as big sister was the target.
She was always the target,
always the line of fire so they didn't have to be.
Didn't have to be something so painful,
but big sister displaced pain.
She is old enough to understand how to go to another place when
reality seemed so unreal.

But her efforts never worked
As daddy's hands slam little girls' bodies into cement walls
As they sit in silence on their little matching bedspreads.
Always sitting in hope, in hope that tomorrow is a new day.

A new day where little girls could try to be good,
Good enough to lie outside, outside in the grass.
And disappear from it all,
because for a moment in time they could
Disappear from step-mom's mean words
Disappear from hair pulling, child shoving,
and window breaking.

Early morning wake ups of screaming in the ears of the little sister in
the top bunk.
Early morning wake ups of puffed wheat cereal in dark kitchen on
cold green benches.

Long days of school where each sister stood by themselves,
as no child of their peers wants to play
with bruised ones that don't eat.
Long days of children laughing at skinny sisters as principals call
them out of class
wondering about the bruises on their faces.

Long nights of sitting on beds
waiting for daddy to get home
So he can find out Principal knows
Principal knows, but just causes more blue bruises
on children's bodies.
Daddy used to say, "This hurts me more than it hurts you."

Daddy you're wrong! Big sister says daddy you're wrong!
I still say daddy you are wrong.
I look back now on what I used to have
The life I used to live and how I felt
You made me feel small and worthless, you left holes in me
Left me with nothing but undernourished childhood
With my last memory of you: crying.

You were crying because you know you're wrong
You left us eight years ago.
Eight years of covering what you did to me,

what you let her do to my little sisters.
So when I say daddy you're wrong,
you better believe it now because I never did.
Until the day three little girls triumphed,
without you.

Fawna Lynn Millwood
December 2003

From Starving to Surviving— and Thriving

12

Of course it took years to get myself back on track. I struggled with personal issues that I could not control or change. My middle school years were the most awkward; I just could not figure out who I was. The constant pressure from my friends and the outside world really affected me, in good ways and bad. I felt trapped some days, as if what happened behind those doors changed me for the worst and there was no turning back. I did things, which I deeply regret, that hurt many people I loved.

Some behaviors I learned while in custody of my father I continued to entertain even into my adolescence. One prominent behavior that I could not control was lying. I did not understand how to get past this. My uncle often scolded me and asked, "Why do you keep lying?" All I could answer was that I didn't know how not to lie. I had spent two years lying to save my own life. I didn't realize that people would have accepted me for who I was. Throughout elementary school and even middle school I lied too many of my friends about so many things. I just wanted to be accepted. I felt like I had to overcompensate for not having real parents or cool clothes.

Looking back now, I hated myself. I hated that I did so many awful things to people who tried to be my friends. I let my interpersonal struggles get the best of me and continued to make decisions that made me lose many of my best friends and people who meant the most to me. For a while I let this fictitious lifestyle consume me, and whole life was a lie. I lied about lying. I never gained the self-confidence all of my friends so easily had. Most people I hurt will never understand why I did what I did. I even let my uncle down so many times.

I felt like the skin I was in was tarnished and just not my own. I felt like I didn't fit in my own skin, or in with any group of friends. I constantly answered the question asked by so many—why do you live with your uncle—with frustration and confusion every time. I loved him but would not forgive him for taking away my opportunity to have a mom and dad. I was thankful he took us away from Benjamin and Diane but I really wanted a mother in my life, especially at this time when I needed her most.

It was all very hard to explain to anyone. How could a child, in a normal conversation, say something like "Well, sit down for an hour and let me tell you about two years of brutal abuse I endured. And let me tell you about how growing up without a mother has affected me, especially while I begin to form romantic relationships." My friends would never understand the anguish caused by growing up trying to copy off an older sister and learning all the things a girl needs to learn to become a woman by myself.

Maybe, in a small way, these situations helps explain: Imagine sitting in the Kohl's dressing room with your uncle asking loudly outside if your "brazier" is too big. I cried as I wished my breasts would grow like the other girls my age and wondered if it was my fault. Or imagine having your embarrassing old-fashioned uncle strictly declining any purchase of a bra in a color other than nude or white. Imagine sneaking off to the feminine hygiene aisle to inconspicuously grab tampons while your uncle adds bread and laundry detergent to the shopping basket. Imagine not having a mother to hold you and stroke your hair as you weep the first time a boy breaks your heart. Try getting away with owning underwear that were anything less than "granny panties."

I'll never forget the first time I wore makeup and my uncle almost had a heart attack. Fawna helped put glitter on my eyes and shiny gloss on my lips for my fifth-grade D.A.R.E graduation and my uncle demanded that I scrub my face before I got back in the car. He grounded me for two weeks when I begged Fawna to pierce my ears and she finally listened. He took away the razors when he learned I was using Fawna's to shave my legs, too. In retrospect I know he was just trying to stop us from growing up too fast. He saw us as beautiful little girls and wanted to keep it that way for as long as he could.

In Elementary School I tried to form friendships, especially because now I was allowed to have friends. The kids my age just didn't understand why I behaved the way I did and why I could not control my emotions. My fifth grade teacher observed a young girl with a lot of baggage but a big drive. She knew from age eleven, right around the time I started writing this book, that I would be able to overcome. The question was just, when and how.

It was during elementary school that I began to grapple with my body image. After living with my uncle for a while, I wasn't as skinny as the other girls my age and the onset of puberty was later than normal. I stuffed my bra in fifth grade, only to become the laughingstock of the whole grade when someone noticed how I was chest-less one day and quite busty the next. The day, when I had to go back wearing just a training bra, was humiliating. As if everyone already didn't know I had stuffed my bra, I had to go back to school proving to them my true figure. I couldn't dare tell Uncle Richard what a stupid and embarrassing thing I had done.

One night in fifth grade my sister wrapped my hair in tight curlers. It was a terrible night of sleep but I felt so pretty in the morning. Bouncy blonde curls grazed my whole head and I wore a pair of prescription glasses I had been saving to show a "new look." It didn't take all of ten minutes to assume a new nickname, "Miss Piggy." One can imagine how this little moniker further deteriorated any positive self-image I had left.

When middle school came around, I joined the swim team and was forced to be in a bathing suit in front of all my peers. I began to skip meals in hopes of looking like some of the popular girls at school. I began to associate the way one looks and how many friends one has. Anorexia was slowly crawling into my life and there was nothing in the way to stop it. In fact, I began to feel so happy that I had many friends and a little attention from boys that I welcomed the disease with open arms.

High school was a life-altering era. In essence, I hated high school. It was awkward yet defining, difficult yet encouraging. But, with the help of my uncle Richard and his refusal to let us feel sorry for ourselves, I was able to change my attitude from "poor me" to let my past make me better, not bitter. A greater power instilled a fire in my heart that lit me up like a firework. I strived for perfection in my schoolwork and decided to be a friend to anyone, because you never know what kind of past someone has had. I continued attempting to gain self-acceptance and continued to write down my memories. I became motivated to be kind and genuinely happy.

Working hard in my studies, accepting nothing less than perfect, I also was able to get involved in a few extracurricular activities and otherwise keep myself busy. I participated in varsity swimming and competed on the varsity gymnastics team. I was in National Honor Society and did 100 hours of community service my senior year.

Most of those activities came about because my uncle made me do them. I didn't want to but he told me I had no choice.

In reflection I realize I did have a choice. He couldn't throw me in the pool at 5 a.m. or do the community service for me. Rather, my good choices were a joint decision. We decided separately, yet in conjunction, that I would not sit at home and feel sorry for myself. It was during this time that I realized that helping people helped me. I learned that helping others gave me a sense of fulfillment and acceptance that I had always longed for. My character soon became respectable and my friendships started to become strong and true. I was reassured with compliments day in and day out from friends, teachers, adults and family members. I felt proud to be going in the right direction.

However, I had a personal conflict in high school that had yet to defeat—my ongoing battle with anorexia and now bulimia. The constant pressure to be thin to have more friends, combined with my activities in sports that required me to wear tight swimsuits or sparkly leotards, was a recipe to allow my eating disorder to grow out of control.

The lack of a mother to constantly reassure me that "you are beautiful the way you are" left me feeling bare and unlikable. Although the night terrors were seldom, they were still occurring and I still continued to struggle with attachment problems and post-traumatic stress. Being able to control how much I weighed was empowering. It felt good to finally have a handle on *something* in my life. Friends came and went, boys rarely showed interest, and I still felt trapped in my own skin. I remembered that my stepmother called me ugly so many times, and her words rang in my head every day. I really did hate myself, that I did something so terrible to my body with a conscious effort. I felt as if I would have to starve myself every day for the rest of my life.

In 2007 a close friend kept urging me to compete for Miss Michigan USA. At first I thought she was crazy and that nobody could ever get me on that stage. One morning in the spring of 2007 I woke up and felt a sudden burst of courage and knew I had to do it. I wasn't sure if I could really get as far as the pageant stage, but I just knew I had to try. I was able to earn several sponsorships from some people who never lost faith in me. I couldn't believe the outpour of support from so many friends, families, and local organizations. Monetary or not, the support was insurmountable. I felt for the first time in my life I had people behind me and would catch me if I fall.

In September of 2008 I competed for Miss Michigan USA and it was an experience that changed my life. I left the pageant filled with confidence, charisma, self-worth, and dreams. I would now be unable to turn back to my past that I so badly wanted to disassociate from but never could. I felt strong enough to stare my stepmother in the face and tell her what a shallow, heartless, and possibly mentally-ill criminal she was. I changed from a lost 9-year-old to a mature and driven 19-year-old in the course of 30 seconds on a brightly lit stage. I was finally able to stand up tall and not let my past define me, but to help make me a better person. That soon became my motto, that my past does not define me, and overcoming is always a possibility, especially if you let it.

On Easter Sunday in 2000, my sisters and I were invited to a large church in our town for the Easter service. I don't know how my uncle got me to go. I do remember I was excited at the prospect of seeing my cousins and aunt who were church members and would be there. It was fun to put on a pretty Easter outfit, and I was moved by the service that explained the resurrection of Jesus and what Easter really means.

The pastor spoke to me that Sunday. He dug deep into my soul and explained not the reason why everything happens but that God has a plan for all of us. It finally made sense to me that although I felt so alone for so long, especially during those horrendous two years, he never left my side. He was there, all my life, and is still next to me now. I began to understand that the reason we went through such hell is all for a purpose. He was using me to be a voice against child abuse and to protect innocent children from harm forever. Spiritually I healed and I finally began to understand why we had the childhood we were given—it was all part of God's plan.

This only helped me continue to find peace with my past. I knew my past would always be a part of me and I would sometimes have to hold back the tears remembering the hurt and sorrow we endured, but I found relief in learning about God and found much comfort in being able to pray to him. I learned to believe in him again, and trust him for any more adversity he may have planned down the road. I also realized that the reason he stood by me and helped me live through that adversity is so that I could live to tell my story and He can use me to help others. I was finally finding true happiness. My eternal relationship with God, the experience at the Miss Michigan pageant, and the people who never gave up on me are the reasons why I have been able to thrive after all odds were against me.

Recovering from my eating disorders was one of my most important personal triumphs. Using the confidence I gained from the pageant and asking God to guide me to a more healthy lifestyle, I was finally able to see my body differently. It took seven long years to make the conscious decision to respect my body, but I finally feel comfortable in my own skin and love me and my body for who I am.

After graduating from high school I went on to graduate with my B.A. in Liberal Studies from the University of Michigan in 2011. During my college years I continued to grow, learn about love and heartbreak, and true friends and fake, and that the key to happiness is to just do the things that make you happy. I worked all the way through school with unending financial and emotional support from Uncle Richard. I enjoy yoga, reading, politics, and traveling. I love my sisters dearly and hope this book gives them the peace I have been so fortunate to find. I am honored that they have allowed me to share our story with you and hope I have not let them down in the telling of it.

The one man in my life to whom I owe unending gratitude, the one who truly rescued my sisters and I, is the man who deserves all the credit. He never gave up on us. After the time in my father's house we really did become those bad kids Diane always said we were. When my uncle took us in we gave him hell. We actually did lie, steal, act out, and defy him. We did the things he specifically asked us not to do. We gave him so much grief. He did his best, the best he knew how to do.

At first he was learning how to take care of us. His discipline was strict at times but it was all he knew. I'll never forget the time he put us all in the corner because one of us had broken something around the house and nobody would confess. I slowly walked into his bedroom to find him sitting on his bed distraught and practically in tears. I could tell he felt frustrated with the type of parenting he had to enforce to keep us in line. I had never seen him like that before. In fact, I had never experienced an adult (other than my mother) expressing such vulnerable emotions.

As I sat next to him and apologized for my bad behavior, I put my head on his shoulder and cried too. I looked over on his nightstand to see a tan book with big black letters laid open and facedown. I read the words, "How to Be a Good Parent." I cried even harder as I realized my sisters and I were all going to have to work together with this man and help each other become a family. We were a family now and always will be.

My uncle utilized every resource possible to make sure we turned out the best we could. He also gave up any possibility for marriage, a social life, even a dedicated work-life. He provided for us the best he could financially, although at times it was really rough. After he adopted us he stopped receiving financial assistance from the State. Now the only money he had to help raise us was his own. Therefore, we never went on family vacations (unless it was a freezing trip skiing up-north, which *was* fun), until our first as a family when I was 15. Even that trip was a tight squeeze, but he gave up a lot to give us a fun memory. He sacrificed everything for us. He put his life on hold to take care of us and give us what little chance we had left at a happy childhood. We spent a lot of rough years living together, trying to figure out who each of us were. My uncle wanted what was best for us but we refused his love and care for years.

It was when the foster care system had failed us for the umpteenth time—when I was almost 12 and we had been living with my uncle for almost three years—that my Uncle Richard stepped in and decided to adopt my sisters and me. I remember hating him for adopting me because that got rid of any chance for me to have a mom and dad. I didn't even know he was thinking of adopting us, and when the social workers gleefully shoved the papers in front of me I was dumbfounded. They all tried to explain he wanted to be responsible for us, forever, and all I cared about was "being normal."

Many people often ask how my sisters and I turned out the way we did. I always silently thank my Uncle Richard and gratefully explain his instrumental role in helping us stay on the right path and make the right choices in life. He was never married and gave up a lucrative job to take in my sisters and me. Yes, I remember resenting him for taking me away from my real dad. I still to this day continuously replay our adoption day in my head. As the social worker ecstatically shouted, "Congratulations!" all I could think was, "Thanks for ruining my life." Twelve years later not only do I not resent him, my uncle has become one of my best friends. Yes, he was strict and his parenting techniques were a little questionable at first, but he learned to love, protect, and support us in the best ways possible, and I'll never be able to thank him enough for his kindness and unconditional love of three girls who needed him more than he knew.

My feelings toward him changed a few years later and I celebrate the fact that I'm adopted. I feel so fortunate to have someone in my life with enough care and love in his heart to "pick me." It was official on Valentine's Day in 2000. What a great day to celebrate the love and care my uncle has for me. Uncle Richard, you are my hero. You are my role model. You saved my life. I would not be the accomplished and strong woman I am today without your constant support and relentless guidance to always do the right thing. You mean more to me than anyone in this world. I would be lost without you.

Every morning when I wake up I look out my window and smile. I am thankful I have a window to look out of. I thank God for the clean sheets I sleep in, the clean and warm clothes I am wearing and the breakfast I am about to eat. I thank him for the life I now have. I couldn't even imagine what my life would be like if I still lived in that terrible home. I believe my sisters and I would not be alive. By leaving that home I was given the opportunity to be someone. Although that transformation took years, I am finally happy in my own skin, have healthy relationships, and still have my sisters. I come from a humble past, and have a promising future. I know that I will be the best mother my future children could ask for. I know that I will give them more love than they can possibly imagine, and they will never experience anything close to the fear and horrors I endured.

Not a day goes by that I don't think about what happened to my sisters and me in that home. Some days it is all I think about. I just take one day at a time. I have learned that it isn't possible to just erase two years out of my life. I can't pretend they didn't happen, because they did. They were dreadful. But they are over. They are in the past. They helped make me who I am today.

It is my every hope to use the injustices that occurred during my own childhood to help those who may need it. I want abused children to feel the power to speak out about the crime he or she is a victim of. Not every adult is a "good grown-up" and there are in fact bad people in this world. If you are being hurt in any way, speak up about it until you find someone who listens.

I want former abused children to feel the strength to retell their stories and become a better person for it. I want foster children to know that maybe their real parents couldn't care for them, but it doesn't mean they aren't loved. Their lives may feel like shambles right now, but if they are lucky enough to be adopted they should hold onto that treasure and never let it go. Bouncing around from home to home can be scary, difficult, and unstable, but it gets easier. There will come a time in your life when you can make the decision to stay in one place forever. Foster children should know that if they are not in a happy, healthy home, there are people who will work very hard to find one for them.

I want parents to know there are better ways to discipline their children than using violence, and there are many resources available to help them. I especially want parents who may have been abused as children to understand that the cycle *can* stop with them. I want social workers to know that although my sisters and I were failed they can still make a difference in the life of a child by just listening and digging deeper. Social workers sometimes need to take their graduate school textbooks and 600-page files and push them aside for a minute. They need to take a step back and look at the situation as a whole. Ask yourself some questions about the situation. Do I really think this home is safe and happy for the child? Do I think there might be something going on and they need help? How can I protect this child? Just use common sense, please, for the sake of innocent children around the world who need you to just think about it. And help.

I want judges to know that sometimes living with the biological parents isn't the best option, because some people are just not meant to be parents. I want those judges to ask the children in private where they want to go and ask why. I want lawmakers to understand that six years is not enough time to heal from the trauma of child abuse and the statute of limitations needs to be increased in Michigan. I also strongly feel that hurting a child is a crime that should be punishable with much stronger consequences than the sentences now outlined by law. Together all of us can make a difference in the life of a child.

Another issue I'd like to address is the common problem of eating disorders. I want young girls (and boys) who may see their body different in the mirror than other people see them to have encouragement and support to recover from this misperception. I will work hard to let those who may have an eating disorder know there is a better life on the other side. A more healthy, more fulfilled life *is* attainable.

I don't want people to feel sorry for me. I feel (and sometimes it helps to repeat this in my head) that there is a reason that I was given the childhood I had. It was hard but I lived through it, specifically to tell my story and help others. Either by God or a power instilled within, I was able to overcome what happened to me, and I want to change the lives of so many and make sure it never happens again.

My road to recovery was long and brutal. At times I wanted to throw in the towel. Some days I would wake up and consciously decide to be uncouth and hate the world. I feel so blessed that I did not continue down that path. Many times I wanted to use my past as an excuse to make bad decisions. The relationships I share with each of my sisters have been tested and torn. These relationships have had their tribulations but they have prevailed. Together we have decided to join with once voice and tell our story because we know it needs to be heard.

In particular, we hope one person hears this story. Not our Uncle Richard, as he knows our unending gratitude and love for him and what he did for us. Not our mother, because she understands—or at least I hope she now understands—why we will be only ever the daughters of one person. Not our father, because he is a coward and knew all of this already, despite his spineless claims he knew nothing. Not the social workers, the teachers, or the principal, because we are humbled and use better judgment than to try to point fingers or gain any compensation from them. All of that is in the past.

We hope the one person who hears this story is the woman who should be in jail for her heinous and merciless crimes. We hope she hears loud and clear that we are still alive, have become incredibly beautiful, and are stronger than ever. She may have spent every day of two years breaking windows, breaking our bones, breaking our hearts, but there is one thing she couldn't break. There is one thing still triumphing over all of this, and it is the bond and the spirit we share as sisters. It is that very spirit we have to thrive together despite her alternate idea of our fate. The one thing she tried for two long, grueling years was to break our spirit, and because we stand tall today she is a failure. She may not have received the proper justice but I strongly feel that by the world reading this book, her justice is served in a different way. Now the world knows what happened behind those walls. Now the world can see the truth. Now everybody understands why we lied then and why we are telling the truth now.

To my beautiful, amazing, mysterious but strong sisters—we did it. Just like the day I looked down at Cam on the bus, I can look at her now with love and hope in my heart and say, Yes, we did it. We made it out alive, and we are stronger today than ever. The bond and our spirits are truly unbreakable, and it is a bond that will be shared forever.

Afterword

As readers are led through the painful, yet inspirational, story of Jasmine, Fawna and Camai, I believe that many are left with a single question: Why didn't Jasmine and her sisters speak up? Why did they actually defend their abusive and dysfunctional caregivers?

The story of the Millwood sisters is not the first dilemma of this sort that we have all heard about on the 6 o'clock news. Anyone who has ever seen the testimony of Elizabeth Smart had to be amazed by her strength and poise in narrating the abuse she experienced at the hands of her captors. Similarly, Jaycee Lee Dugard presents herself as a composed and able 31-year-old mother, despite being held victimized for 18 years of her life. And now we have just read the story of a beautiful, educated and talented young woman, Jasmine, who graduated from the University of Michigan and is nowhere near slowing down.

Ironically, the positive presence and functionality of these three sisters makes us even more mystified. It goes back to the question of how and why they were able to be so successfully manipulated by their captors. Clinicians can point to diagnoses such as PTSD (Post Traumatic Stress Disorder) or discuss the "Stockholm Syndrome" (the phenomenon in which the victim bonds with their captor for survival) in the search for an explanation. But these diagnoses, these labels, simply describe the behavior; they do not account for it. While we may be inclined to focus on the question of why these women could not flee sooner, the more important question should be how they survived their abuse and managed to remain intact.

Frankly, I do not believe that any treatment professional can fully explain the indomitable spirit that allowed the Millwood girls to prevail when so many others, understandably, would not have.

There is a psychological term that describes but, as I said before, cannot account for the perseverance of such victims. They are referred to as "invulnerables." These individuals might be described as "bulletproof," as "Teflon people" or just simply survivors. Whatever the term of choice, it describes individuals who have endured terrible circumstances and somehow managed to continue with their lives successfully.

I met Jasmine three years ago, and anyone who knows her would not picture her to be the victim of the events that her book relates. And yet, I learned all of it to be true, as my review of her case records demonstrated recently. Hopefully, the existence of such cases will diminish as our society becomes more skilled at identifying and supporting women like Jasmine and her sisters.

But the purpose of this note is not to assign blame. Rather it is to celebrate the strength and tenacity of those "Invulnerables" and to admire the courage that their resilience demonstrates. All of us should be so blessed as to survive as they have.

Jasmine's life and her survival demonstrate how, with the intervention of one caring individual (in her case, her Uncle Richard), a life can be reclaimed.

Can we be that person for another child?

John V. Farrar Ed.D., LPC
snowmantherapy.com

Resources

For more information about the organizations that a portion of the proceeds of this book will benefit:

St. Clair County Child Abuse & Neglect Council
www.sccstopchildabuse.org

YMCA Storer Camps, Jackson Michigan
www.ymcastorercamps.org

For additional information about organizations that serve to protect children, raise awareness about child abuse, and help improve the foster care system:

CARE House of Oakland County
www.carehouse.org

Childhelp
www.childhelp.org

Child Welfare League of America
www.cwla.org

Michigan's Children
www.michiganschildren.org

National Child Abuse Hotline:
1-800-4-A-CHILD

Orchards Children's Services
www.orchards.org

Prevent Child Abuse America
www.preventchildabuse.org

Save The Children
www.savethechildren.org

The Center for Prevention of Abuse
www.centerforpreventionofabuse.org

U.S. Department of Health & Human Services
Administration for Children & Families
www.acf.hhs.gov

CPSIA information can be obtained at www.ICGtesting.com
Printed in the USA
BVOW061229120312

284900BV00003B/2/P